ADAPT

Advancing Decision Making and Problem Solving for Teens

JASON BURROW-SÁNCHEZ, PH.D.

© 2013 JASON BURROW-SÁNCHEZ, PH.D.

The purchasing school administrator or educator is granted permission to use and reproduce the reproducible forms and files provided on the CD solely for the purpose of implementing the ADAPT program. Except as expressly permitted above and under the United States Copyright Act of 1976, no materials in this work may be used, reproduced, or distributed in any form or by any means, electronic or mechanical, without the prior written consent of the publisher.

Any resources and website addresses are provided for reader convenience and were current at the time of publication. Report any broken links to info@pacificnwpublish.com.

Published in the United States by
Pacific Northwest Publishing
2451 Willamette St.
Eugene, Oregon 97405
www.pacificnwpublish.com

ISBN: 978-1-59909-052-8

Cover by Aaron Graham
Book design and layout by Natalie Conaway

Eugene, Oregon | www.pacificnwpublish.com

*This book is dedicated to my wife, Jen,
and daughters, Emory and Tatum.
Thank you for always providing your love,
support, and encouragement!*

CONTENTS

About the Author vii

Acknowledgments ix

Section 1: Overview

Section 1.1 Introduction 1

Section 1.2 Background 8

Section 2: Important Considerations

Section 2.1 Facilitating Groups 11

Section 2.2 Student Characteristics and Cultural Issues 16

Section 2.3 Logistics 19

Section 2.4 School Support and Buy-In 20

Section 2.5 Ethical and Legal Issues 23

Section 2.6 Connecting With Parents/Guardians 26

Section 2.7 Collecting Data and Evaluating Outcomes 29

Section 3: How Sessions Work

Section 3.1 Session Structure 33

Section 3.2 Practice Sheets 36

Section 3.3 Group Development Across Sessions 39

Section 4: Session Plans

Session 1 Introduction to ADAPT: Positive Outcomes Through
Problem Solving and Decision Making 43

Session 2 How Do I Solve Problems? The 4-Ws Problem-
Solving Model 57

Session 3 Why Do Things Happen to Me? Decision-Making Chains . . . 73

Session 4 Why Do I Do That? Part I. Mapping and Understanding
Problem Behaviors 87

v

CONTENTS

Session 5 Why Do I Do That? Part II.
Mapping Alternative Behaviors 99

Session 6 What Are Drugs and What Do They Do? 111

Session 7 How Do I Refuse Drugs?
Triggers, Communication, Reasons 127

Session 8 How Do I Communicate Better With Others?
Assertive Communication Skills. 141

Session 9 How Do I Manage My Anger?. 159

Session 10 How Do I Manage My Negative Mood? 175

Session 11 How Do I Get the Support I Need From Others? 193

Session 12 Ending the Program and Additional Support 205

Research Summary 215

References 219

ABOUT THE AUTHOR

Jason Burrow-Sánchez, Ph.D.

Jason Burrow-Sánchez, Ph.D., is Associate Professor of Counseling Psychology in the Department of Educational Psychology at the University of Utah. He earned his doctorate in Counseling Psychology at the University of Oregon in 2003. His research areas include the prevention and treatment of substance abuse in adolescent populations in school and community settings, with a particular interest in Latino adolescents. His program of research has been funded at the local, state and national levels. He has published numerous articles and book chapters and is the senior author of the book *Helping Students Overcome Substance Abuse: Effective Practices for Prevention and Intervention*. In addition, he is a licensed psychologist in the State of Utah.

ACKNOWLEDGMENTS

I want to acknowledge and thank the people who worked on and contributed to the Building and Enhancing Skills for Teens (BEST) Program (which the ADAPT program is based on) during its two-year (2007–2009) development and testing period. In alphabetical order, they are: Dr. Mandy Allison, Angela Bennett, Megan Call, Sarah Clarke-Smith, Yecenia Gomez, Adriana Lopez, and Megan Wrona. I would also like to thank the high school students, school personnel, and parents who participated in the program and taught the members of our team many invaluable lessons about conducting interventions in a school setting. The following funding sources provided resources to develop and test the BEST program: Department of Pediatrics at the University of Utah (Adolescent Health Initiative Grant), Utah State Office of Education, and the American Academy of Pediatrics (Healthy People 2010 Grant).

Thanks go to the people who encouraged me to get this work from draft to publication. First, I want to thank Dr. William Jenson for encouraging me to publish this work in the first place and for his continued support during the process. Thanks, Bill! Second, thanks to everyone at Pacific Northwest Publishing, especially Dan, Marilyn, Natalie, and Sara! Your detailed feedback on drafts and overall continued support of the project were much appreciated. You are a great group of folks to work with! Third, I want to thank the undergraduate and graduate students I have worked with on this and other intervention projects at the University of Utah. Your ideas, inspiration, hard work, and dedication contribute immensely to the intervention work we conduct and help us find what best works to improve the lives of adolescents and families.

Finally, thanks to my family—Jen, Emory, and Tatum—for putting up with me during many long days, late nights, and early morning writing sessions. Jen, thanks for being there to discuss the project, review drafts, and provide great ideas and suggestions throughout this process. Girls, thanks for providing the "sweet treats" that kept me going and for reminding me to take breaks (whether I wanted to or not) from writing. All your love, encouragement, and patience helped make this book a reality!

OVERVIEW

SECTION 1

Introduction

What is ADAPT?

Advancing Decision Making and Problem Solving for Teens (ADAPT) is a cognitive-behavioral intervention that combines components of social learning theory to provide teens with a program that teaches, reinforces, and supports the development of fundamental decision-making and problem-solving skills. ADAPT also teaches strategies for dealing with the common adolescent problems of aggression, depressive moods, and substance use.

Adolescents who are effective at problem solving and decision making tend to experience fewer problem behaviors. Misbehavior often results from a lack of these fundamental skills. By improving problem-solving and decision-making skills, ADAPT promotes the positive behavior and good mental health that allows students to cope in many different situations.

ADAPT lessons are delivered over a 12-week period. School professionals such as school counselors, school psychologists, social workers, and other qualified school mental health personnel facilitate the 45- to 60-minute sessions with small groups of 8 to 10 students. This small-group format gives students the opportunity to learn and practice skills in an environment where they can receive feedback from their peers.

Who might benefit?

ADAPT is designed for middle school and high school students who need secondary or selected preventive interventions. These are students at risk for developing more serious problem behaviors. Figure 1 on the following page (Mrazek & Haggerty, 1994; Walker et al., 1996) shows where ADAPT fits within a typical RTI three-tiered model of intervention.

SECTION 1.1 INTRODUCTION

Figure 1
ADAPT's place in the RTI intervention model

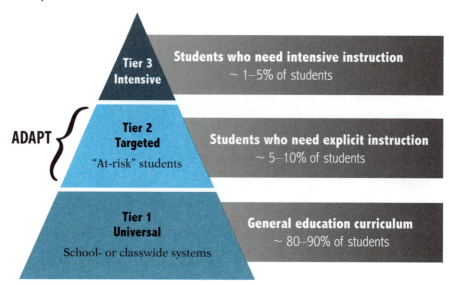

Compared with universal and intensive preventive interventions, selecting students for a targeted intervention can be difficult. Generally, no selection criteria are needed for a universal intervention because it is delivered to a general population, such as an entire class or school. At the other end of the continuum, selecting students who need an intensive intervention is relatively straightforward for the simple reason that these students typically display high rates of problem behavior. School faculty and administrators may find themselves spending much of their time working with these students to address their problem behaviors. However, students who require targeted interventions typically do not display consistent problem behavior; it is usually more intermittent. These students may go unnoticed because their behavior does not seem as severe compared with the students who require intensive interventions. Although selection criteria for ADAPT may not be obvious, you can use the following sources to help identify students who would benefit from ADAPT.

- Referrals from counselors or teachers who have direct contact with students and have observed problem behavior
- Referrals from concerned parents who have observed problem behavior
- Self-referrals from students who are exhibiting problem behavior
- Referrals based on the Risk Factor Referral Checklist (Reproducible A-1, available on the CD)

What specific skills are taught in ADAPT?

ADAPT is set up so that students work on cognitive processes and specific behavioral skills in each session. Skills taught later in the program build on the fundamental problem-solving and decision-making skills taught at the beginning of the program.

The sessions in ADAPT are:

Session 1
Introduction to ADAPT
Positive Outcomes Through Decision Making and Problem Solving

This session introduces students to ADAPT. Students begin to get to know each other, learn more about the program, and go over group expectations, issues of confidentiality, and the group contract.

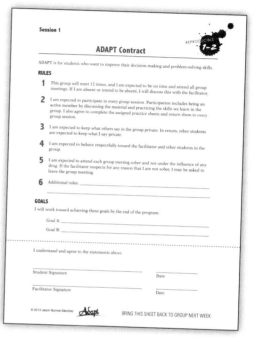

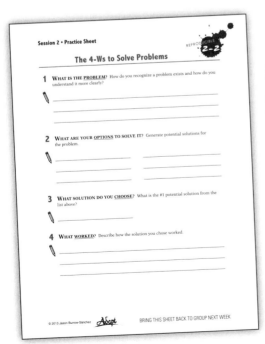

Session 2
How Do I Solve Problems?
The 4-Ws Problem-Solving Model

Students learn and practice how to resolve problems by recognizing and clarifying the problem, identifying options to solve it, selecting a solution, and then determining whether the solution worked.

SECTION 1.1 **INTRODUCTION**

Session 3
Why Do Things Happen to Me?
Decision-Making Chains

By using a decision-making chain, students learn how small and seemingly unimportant decisions can lead to big problems. Then students learn how alternative decision-making strategies can lead to better outcomes.

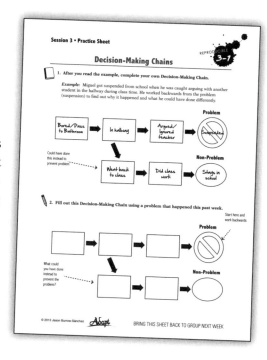

Session 4
Why Do I Do That? Part I
Mapping and Understanding Problem Behaviors

Students learn to identify triggers (antecedents) that lead to problem behaviors that in turn result in negative consequences.

Session 5
Why Do I Do That? Part II
Mapping Alternative Behaviors

Students learn to identify triggers and then replace problem behaviors with positive alternatives. This session encourages students to engage in positive behaviors by helping them understand that positive behaviors lead to positive consequences.

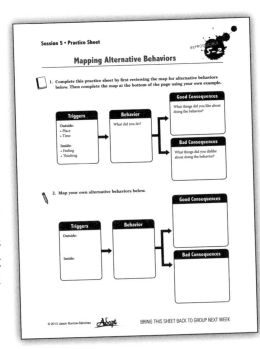

Section 1: Overview

Session 6
What Are Drugs and What Do They Do?

Students often receive inaccurate information about the physical and psychological effects of drug use. In this session, students learn facts about the effects of drug use to aid them in making better decisions.

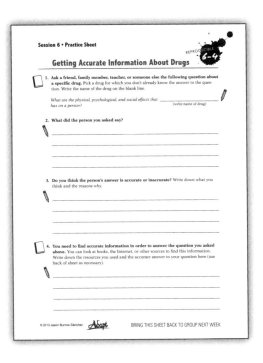

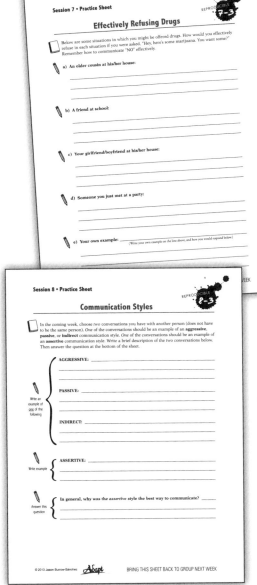

Session 7
How Do I Refuse Drugs?

It can be difficult for teens to refuse drugs because of things such as peer pressure. Students learn why drug refusal can be difficult and ways to overcome those obstacles.

Session 8
How Do I Communicate Better With Others?
Assertive Communication Skills

Students learn the importance of good communication skills as well as how to use I-messages and good listening skills.

ADAPT: Advancing Decision Making and Problem Solving for Teens 5

SECTION 1.1 INTRODUCTION

Session 9
How Do I Manage My Anger?

Everyone experiences anger, but not everyone expresses anger appropriately. Students learn specific skills to help them recognize and manage their anger in appropriate ways that lead to better outcomes.

Session 10
How Do I Manage My Negative Mood?

Negative moods are normal but can become problematic when they last for long periods of time. Students learn specific skills to help them recognize and manage negative or depressive moods. *Note:* This session is not a treatment for depression. If you suspect clinical or major depression, facilitate a referral for appropriate assessment and treatment.

Session 11
How Do I Get the Support I Need From Others?

Students learn that support from others, such as advice or encouragement, will help them deal with difficult situations more successfully. Students learn skills for identifying and obtaining social support from the people in their lives.

Section 1: Overview

Session 12
Ending the Program and Additional Support

In this final session, students review skills they have learned and celebrate goals accomplished over the course of the program. Students also learn strategies for obtaining additional support after the program has ended.

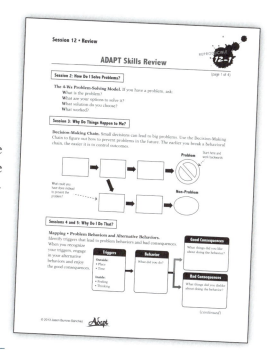

Why are the skills taught in ADAPT important?

Social science research indicates that students who are better at problem solving and decision making are less likely to exhibit problem behaviors. Because of a combination of environment and biology, some adolescents are better at these fundamental skills whereas others need more direct instruction to improve these skills. Medical research has also found that our brains do not fully develop until our mid-20s, and the last portion of the brain to develop is the part involved in decision making and problem solving; that is why these skills are not fully developed in adolescents and why teaching them is so important.

Research also indicates that teaching the fundamental skills of decision making and problem solving *together with* teaching strategies for dealing with specific problem behaviors is generally more effective than just addressing a specific problem behavior (see Table 1-1 for an example).

This is exactly what ADAPT does. It teaches adolescents how to improve their problem-solving and decision-making skills within the context of managing specific behavioral issues. ADAPT also teaches the complementary skills of effective communication and obtaining support from others.

> **If drug use is a problem:**
> - Teaching drug refusal is effective.
> - Teaching drug refusal <u>and</u> problem solving and decision making is even more effective.

TABLE 1-1
Addressing Drug Issues Example

Specific Skill	+ Fundamental Skills	= Outcome
Drug Refusal		= Effective
Drug Refusal	+ Problem Solving & Decision Making	= More Effective

SECTION 1.2

Background

How was ADAPT developed, and how does it work?

ADAPT was developed on a foundation of cognitive-behavioral and social learning theory principles. Cognitive-behavioral therapy focuses on improving fundamental skills deficits in order to decrease problem behaviors and increase positive behaviors. Social learning theory indicates that adolescents learn behaviors, both good and bad, from models in their environment. Taken together, these theories suggest that adolescents who have skill deficits that lead to problem behaviors may have learned them, in part, through observing models in their environments but that these deficits can be addressed through interventions that teach or model more functional problem-solving and decision-making skills. This is how ADAPT works. It teaches students functional decision-making and problem-solving skills that address skill deficits and help reduce the risk of problem behaviors.

ADAPT translates these intervention strategies for use in a school-based prevention program that targets multiple problem behaviors. Individual problem behaviors, such as substance abuse, do not occur in a vacuum but rather in concert with other problem behaviors. One behavior can compound or even create another problem behavior. For example, a student who is feeling down might start using drugs in an attempt to feel better. This, in turn, might cause her to start doing poorly in school. By addressing skill deficits and improving fundamental skills, ADAPT may help to reduce the risk of other problem behaviors—behaviors such as delinquency, low self-esteem, and poor school performance.

ADAPT was developed and tested during a two-year randomized wait-list control pilot study with 80 at-risk students in a high school setting. The goals for pilot testing included establishing procedures for recruitment and retention, measuring social validity (for example, participant satisfaction), and examining indicators of efficacy.

The distribution of students across grade levels (9–12) and gender was fairly even during both years of the study. Approximately 60% of the students across both years reported racial/ethnic backgrounds other than White, with the largest non-White subgroup being Hispanic/Latino.

Outcomes of the pilot study include:

- Satisfaction scores across both years were generally high for students, teachers, and parents. Most participants found the program worth their time and effort and would recommend it to others.
- Well over half of the intervention students reported abstaining from alcohol and marijuana in the month prior to the end of the intervention (*Note*: Comparison with control group for this outcome was not possible; see the Research Summary on p. 215 for more detailed information).
- On average, intervention students reported fewer depressive symptoms at post-test across both years compared with students in the control group. More specifically, students in the intervention reported fewer depressive symptoms than approximately 60% of those in the control group.
- On average, students in the intervention group reported higher self-esteem scores at post-test across both years than students in the control condition. More specifically, students in the intervention reported higher self-esteem scores than approximately 70% of those in the control group.

The results from the two-year pilot study were very promising, indicating that students who participated in the intervention generally had better outcomes than those in the control condition. Students, teachers, and parents perceived the program to be worthwhile and helpful. In addition, school personnel positively embraced the program, which helped generate student referrals and sustainability over the two-year development and testing period. (For more detailed information on this study, see the Research Summary on p. 215.)

IMPORTANT CONSIDERATIONS

SECTION 2

2.1 Facilitating Groups

Who can facilitate ADAPT groups?

A range of school professionals, including school counselors, school psychologists, social workers, and other qualified school mental health personnel can facilitate ADAPT groups. Before facilitating a group, make sure you've studied Sections 1–4 and are familiar with each ADAPT session. A facilitator can make or break a group, so it is essential to be well versed in how ADAPT works. If you are a first-time facilitator, make sure you have access to a mentor or senior colleague with experience conducting groups who can provide support and guidance during the course of the program.

What is the "big picture" for facilitating ADAPT groups?

School professionals who implement ADAPT should keep two "big picture" ideas in mind when facilitating groups. Successful facilitation requires consideration of group management and material coverage. Both aspects are equally important and should be considered in concert.

Group management refers to all of the leadership and behavior management issues that you must take into account when facilitating a group. This includes understanding how groups develop as a working unit across time, displaying effective leadership skills, and knowing when and how to implement behavior management strategies for group members.

SECTION 2.1 **FACILITATING GROUPS**

Material coverage refers to your knowledge and skill in regard to the session topic and how you teach this information to students. Keep in mind that your knowledge and skill in facilitating ADAPT will increase as you implement the program.

What group leadership skills are needed to facilitate a group?

It is important that you demonstrate effective group leadership skills to the students in the group. Most adolescents can easily detect when an adult does not seem confident, knowledgeable, or skilled in performing a particular task. Facilitating a group is no exception. Listed below are essential tasks you must become adept at in order to be an effective group leader.

1 Build rapport with students.
From the start of the program, work on building rapport with students. If you have genuine interest in and concern for the students in your group, you will have no problem doing this. Here are several ways you can develop rapport with students:

- Express appropriate interest in the students' lives. For example, ask about their experiences in school, favorite sports, and hobbies.
- Express concern about the students' well-being.
- Listen to student concerns and address them as needed.
- Make sure you are consistent so that students know what to expect.
- Emphasize that what students say is important.
- Use appropriate humor.

This list of examples is not exhaustive. It is important for you to build rapport with students in ways that fit your style and who you are. By effectively developing rapport from the beginning of the program, you can establish an effective working relationship with students even when the relationship is strained (see #6 below).

2 Use basic communication skills.
Basic communication skills are important for building effective working relationships with students. These skills include actively listening to students, using closed- and open-ended questions effectively for information gathering, and paraphrasing and summarizing what students have said. Use these skills to help students in the group feel heard and understood—a novel experience for many at-risk students in a school setting.

12   *Section 2: Important Considerations*

3 **Display confidence and a willingness to learn.**
It is important to display confidence when leading the group sessions, even if this is your first time doing so. Students quickly sense when adults lack confidence in performing a task, which could lead them to challenge your leadership role. You need to balance a confident demeanor with a willingness to learn from the students in the group. Achieving this balance will place students more at ease and boost your ability to build effective working relationships with students in the group.

4 **Display knowledge of group topics.**
Become familiar with the material in ADAPT prior to leading your first group. Students will have more confidence in you if you display some command of the material rather than learning it for the first time with them. Read through the entire manual before implementing ADAPT, try the activities, and make sure that you understand all components of the program.

5 **Provide structure for the group.**
Provide students with structure and organization to increase their confidence in your leadership skills and to improve their overall view of the program. Most people do not want to spend their time doing something that is poorly structured and disorganized. In fact, most students appreciate a program that is highly structured (whether they admit it or not!) because they know what to expect. Your ability to structure the session will make students feel more comfortable. Utilize the structure and organization already built into ADAPT to achieve this goal.

6 **Work with resistant members.**
Some students are apt to express resistance to being in the program. Student resistance is more likely to occur during the first few group sessions. Students may express resistance to being in an ADAPT group in different ways. They may resist verbally ("I don't want to be here," "This is a waste of time," "I won't get anything out of this") or nonverbally (showing up late, wanting to leave early, taking excessive bathroom breaks, not participating in sessions).

Address resistance in an appropriate manner rather than ignore it. Some of the most useful strategies for dealing with student resistance are based on principles of motivational interviewing (Miller & Rollnick, 2002). In general, the most effective way to address resistance is to ask the student specifically what he or she doesn't like about being in the group so you

ADAPT: Advancing Decision Making and Problem Solving for Teens **13**

SECTION 2.1 FACILITATING GROUPS

can understand and address those issues. Don't place blame on the student for not wanting to be in the group. In fact, blaming the student will serve only to increase the student's level of resistance. The following is an example of a response that is more likely to facilitate communication with the student than to shut it down.

John, you have said three or four times that you are bored in the group sessions and don't feel like they are useful. I want to make sure I understand what you are saying. I want everyone in the group to feel like they are getting something out of our sessions.

I also want you to know that I wouldn't want to be in a group that I felt was a waste of time. Can you explain what you mean by giving me some examples? If they are things we can improve, let's discuss that also.

This type of response demonstrates to the student and others in the group that you take their concerns seriously, that you are willing to listen, and that you are open to making changes that improve their experience. Responses that shut down communication include such things as:

- *I don't really care what you think. You have to be in this group.*
- *You are the only one making those complaints. No one else is, so things must be OK.*
- *You just need to get with the program and shape up.*

(See Burrow-Sánchez & Hawken [2007] for specific suggestions on working with resistant members in school-based groups.)

7 **Be aware of and competent in dealing with cultural issues.**
Schools are constantly becoming more diverse in terms of race and ethnicity. The cultural issues you face will in part depend on the demographic composition of the schools you work in. Refer to Section 2.2 for detailed information about cultural awareness and competency.

8 **Encourage ownership of the group.**
When students have a sense of ownership in the group, it will increase their investment and participation in the sessions and what they learn from them. Begin to instill a feeling of ownership during the first session by telling students that the group belongs to them. Keep reminding students that they can influence their own experiences during group sessions. Emphasize that students will have some control over what they get out of the program. To foster a sense of ownership throughout the program, invite students to share their experiences with the group.

14   *Section 2: Important Considerations*

9 **Maintain appropriate boundaries.**
Make sure that you maintain appropriate boundaries with students. Building rapport requires getting to know the students, but this should be done in an appropriate manner that does not involve delving too deeply into their personal lives. Work toward being a good facilitator rather than a friend, parent, or confidant. Start the program with firm, clear boundaries and then relax them appropriately during the course of the program. It is difficult to try to establish firm boundaries after you have already established more relaxed boundaries.

10 **Be a good role model for behavior.**
One of the most important things to keep in mind when facilitating a group is that you are a role model for students in the group. Students will use their observations of your behavior to determine norms for interacting in the group. If you are sarcastic, demeaning, or dismissive, students will assume they can act this way also. But if you display appropriate interpersonal skills and boundaries, students will perceive that this is how they should behave in the group. An attitude of "Do as I say and not as I do" does not work. What does work is to "practice what you preach."

(See Erford, 2010; Geroski & Kraus, 2010; and Greenburg, 2003 for additional information on group management.)

Is additional training available?

If potential facilitators in your district would benefit from additional training with a skilled implementer, call 1-866-542-1490 for more information.

ADAPT: Advancing Decision Making and Problem Solving for Teens   **15**

SECTION 2.2 Student Characteristics and Cultural Issues

What are important student issues to consider?

Depending on your school setting, groups may be made up of students with varied backgrounds and characteristics. To facilitate a group successfully, you need to account for these differences as you proceed through the program. ADAPT has been designed with this in mind. In fact, you are encouraged to modify sessions to meet both student needs and the needs of your school setting. Following are some of the important characteristics and cultural issues you will need to consider.

Age

The range of student ages in each group will vary depending on your particular school. For instance, students in some high schools range in age from 14 to 18. Because the cognitive abilities of a 14-year-old are different from those of an 18-year-old, you would need to modify the material so that everyone in the group can benefit. Alternatively, a group from a school with a larger population or one that serves fewer grade levels may allow you to group students with a smaller range in ages. In this case, your sessions may need little to no modification to address this issue.

Gender

The program material in ADAPT is designed to be general enough so you can address issues for both genders. However, it may be beneficial to slightly modify the material to fit the gender composition of particular groups. For example, if the majority of students in a group are male, you might spend more time talking about externalizing behavioral issues such as aggression, whereas with a majority of female students you might spend more time on internalizing behavioral issues such as mood management and interpersonal relations.

Cultural Background

As a school professional, you already know that today's students are increasingly diverse both culturally and linguistically. The racial and ethnic makeup of your groups, along with such factors as the type of school (for example, public, private, charter), affluence of the community, and region of the country, will affect how students interact with the ADAPT materials. In order to work effectively with groups of diverse students, you must be culturally fluent—that is, you must have knowledge of and respect for the various cultural traditions of your students.

Section 2: Important Considerations

Use the following three guidelines to help ensure that you are culturally fluent and have the skills needed to work with a diverse group of students (Burrow-Sánchez & Hawken, 2007; Sue et al., 1998).

1 **Be aware of your own cultural background.**

Most people identify with at least one particular cultural background. These cultural backgrounds come with beliefs, values, biases, and stereotypes that influence the cultural lens through which we see the world. It's important to understand how your own cultural background affects your attitudes and how you interact with others. For example, a belief in being individually oriented might be an acceptable and even a valued trait for someone from a European American background, but might not be culturally congruent for someone from a culture in which collectivism and reciprocity are valued. If you understand your own cultural background, you will be more open and able to understand students from other cultural backgrounds.

2 **Be knowledgeable about your students' cultural backgrounds.**

Be aware of the various cultural backgrounds that your students come from and realize that these students may or may not share the same beliefs, values, and biases. For instance, if you work in a typical public school in Chicago, you might have large populations of African American and Latino students. If you work in a public school in Oklahoma, you might have a number of Native American students. If you work in a small, rural community in Montana, you might have a more homogenous group of students from mostly European American backgrounds. Though it isn't necessary to be fluent in all these cultures, it is important to be knowledgeable about the specific cultural traits of the students in your school and to have the skills needed to address them.

3 **Be knowledgeable about culturally congruent techniques, strategies, and interventions.**

Understand the cultural congruence, or lack thereof, between interventions and students' backgrounds. Many of the intervention programs used in schools today have been developed from the perspective of European American culture. That is, they're based on "mainstream" cultural values and beliefs and need to be adapted for use with students from different cultural backgrounds. For example, ADAPT Session 8 is about teaching students how to communicate assertively with others, which includes being direct and using eye contact. Although assertiveness is preferred in the European American culture, it is not congruent with all cultures. For instance, a Latino student who uses these skills with a parent may

ADAPT: Advancing Decision Making and Problem Solving for Teens **17**

SECTION 2.2 STUDENT CHARACTERISTICS AND CULTURAL ISSUES

be seen as disrespectful, even though these skills are acceptable in an American school context. In this case, it is important to discuss differences with the group and talk about the most appropriate way to communicate assertively with a Latino parent.

Myriad cultural issues could arise in different groups across school settings, so it is important for you to use your best judgment in making cultural adaptations while adhering to the overall structure of ADAPT. Facilitators who understand and integrate cultural issues into their group material are more likely to successfully meet the needs of the students in their groups.

Modifying ADAPT to account for different student characteristics and cultural backgrounds is an essential factor in your ability to build rapport, empathy, and understanding with the students in your group. You may also find that, despite the challenges involved in working with a diverse group of students, the experience is not only rewarding but a great learning opportunity as well.

Customization Tips

- When explaining and discussing the skills and concepts covered in ADAPT, use examples generated by students in the group whenever possible.

- If students are reluctant to suggest examples themselves, select examples that are relevant to students in your group.

- In past experience with ADAPT, drug-use scenarios have proven to be relevant to many of the students in the program. Provocative questions such as "Why do people do drugs?" promote engagement because most students will want to respond with their own ideas. Other topics that may engage group members include getting into fights, skipping school/class, or leaving when arguing with parents.

- When discussing drug use, focus on the drugs that students in your group and school are most likely to use.

- If you use the sample scenarios provided in the session plans, change names, issues, and other details to better suit the needs of your students and school setting. For example, in a high school with a high proportion of Latino students, you would not want to use all Anglo names when presenting examples.

- Use the vocabulary and terminology students in the group use. For example, before you discuss managing anger and negative moods (Sessions 9 and 10), ask students how they describe these feelings.

18   *Section 2: Important Considerations*

Logistics

SECTION 2.3

How do you schedule groups, and where do you hold meetings?

Develop a plan for program implementation that takes into account the established school schedule and space available.

1 How long do group sessions last?
Group sessions may last anywhere from 45 to 60 minutes—with 60 minutes being optimal. If your sessions are closer to 45 minutes, add one or two sessions to the program so you end up with 13 or 14 sessions instead of 12. If your group meets during school hours, sessions may need to coincide with class periods. In that case, modify the duration of sessions to fit within your school's established class periods.

2 How often do groups meet?
Groups meet once a week over the course of the 12-week program. However, you can adjust the group schedule as needed. For example, groups could meet twice a week, which would shorten the overall program to six weeks. (In this case, you need to modify practice sheet assignments so they can be completed in a shorter time period.) You may also wish to lengthen the program to make up time when the program is suspended over school breaks (for example, winter break, spring break). The most important variable is to schedule groups in a consistent manner that minimizes breaks between sessions.

Optional Booster Session: A booster session is an opportunity for you to check in with students at a predetermined date after the regular 12-week program has ended. If you choose to include a booster session, consider the following guidelines:

- If possible, plan and schedule the booster session at the beginning of the program rather than after your group is already in progress. It is important that all students in the group are aware of the booster session and invited to attend.
- Schedule the booster session approximately one month after program completion. If needed, schedule a second booster session a month after the first one. Try to schedule the booster sessions in the same location where regular sessions were held.
- Use the booster session as an opportunity to check in with students and help them generalize the skills they learned in the program to obtain the types of support available to them in the school or community.

ADAPT: Advancing Decision Making and Problem Solving for Teens

SECTION 2.3 **LOGISTICS**

3 **When should groups be scheduled?**
Attendance is usually best when group sessions take place during school hours. Try to reduce the amount of time students will miss from any particular class. For example, consider having students miss the end of one class and the beginning of another. If you can avoid having students miss all or most of any one class, you will have greater staff support.

If scheduling groups during school hours is not an option, consider the following recommendations for an after-school program:

- To maximize attendance, schedule groups as soon after school ends as possible. The longer the length of time between the end of the school day and the start of group, the less likely students will be to attend.
- Decrease the distance students have to travel to attend the group by facilitating groups on school grounds rather than at an off-site location.

4 **Where should groups meet?**
A dedicated space lends credibility to the program and makes it more likely that students, faculty, and staff will view the program as important. If possible, hold groups in the same location (for example, a specific class or meeting room) for the duration of the program. Your meeting place should offer a reasonable level of privacy and also be relatively free from distractions (for example, not next to the music room).

It's worth the time and effort to arrange a stable location at the school. This will help students take ownership of the program, focus on the purpose of group instead of having to find a new location every session, and provide a sense of stability. It will also give you an opportunity to have a more organized space to store materials and set up sessions.

5 **Will course credit be an option?**
Besides holding groups during school, you can also improve attendance by providing students with course credit or course make-up credit. If a course-credit option is used, clearly explain to students what the expectations are for earning credit. For example, you might establish that 80% attendance is equal to full credit.

Determining the logistics of the program sometimes requires patience and flexibility. Implementing the program will become easier the more times you do it. Eventually, you will get the bugs worked out. The bottom line is that you must find the schedule that works best for your school setting and your students.

School Support and Buy-In

SECTION 2.4

How do you get the school and staff to support the ADAPT program?

Before implementing ADAPT, you will need approval from the school administration and support from staff. Support for implementing new programs should begin with the school administrators. It has become increasingly important in school settings to justify actions and demonstrate that programs work.

Discuss the following with administrators:

- The need for ADAPT
- How ADAPT can serve students in your school
- Skills taught
- Ways to monitor and evaluate outcomes (see Section 2.7)

Along with the support and approval of the administration, obtain support and buy-in from school staff. Present ADAPT at a faculty meeting so you can share the benefits of the program and address potential staff concerns, such as students missing class to attend the program and how the program will affect the regular school day. Staff buy-in at the outset of the program will help you manage short-term potential concerns and help maintain the long-term sustainability of the program.

Staff buy-in makes scheduling easier. It is important for teachers to understand the potential long-term benefits of ADAPT in terms of greater school success for participants. A common concern for teachers with students who are already struggling is how to balance the need for out-of-class programming with the student's need to be in class. You will need to answer the following question for teachers: "What advantage does participation in ADAPT have for an academically struggling student when missing class is part of the program?" Thinking of an answer to this question beforehand will help you when negotiating with teachers about group scheduling. Of course, the answer to this question will partly depend on the needs of the students in your school. For example, in an alternative school setting the answer to this question may be more obvious to school staff because they see the benefit for students to participate in programming that will improve their fundamental problem-solving and decision-making capacities. In traditional school settings, however, the benefit of student participation may be less obvious. In this case, you will need to engage and educate school staff on what ADAPT can provide.

Your response to these types of teacher concerns should be genuine and accommodating. You should really listen to the concerns teachers have as opposed to brushing them off (for example, "That teacher always complains").

ADAPT: Advancing Decision Making and Problem Solving for Teens

SECTION 2.4 **SCHOOL SUPPORT AND BUY-IN**

Validate the concerns you hear and find out if they are common among teachers. This will give you an idea of the range of concerns you need to address. Also ask teachers for their suggestions on how to address the concerns raised. You might ask such things as, "How can we address your concern and also allow the student to participate in the program?" or "What do you suggest in this situation?" Inform teachers that you will check in with them periodically throughout the program (and make sure you do so!) to monitor their concerns and determine how things are working.

Finally, keep the lines of communication open with teachers, which will help you to recruit them as allies for the program. Usually, most teacher concerns can effectively be solved using the guidelines above. Keep in mind that some of the most resistant teachers at the beginning of the program can become some of the most ardent supporters if you effectively engage them.

Ethical and Legal Issues

SECTION
2.5

What ethical and legal issues do you need to know?

Before starting an ADAPT group, you need to be aware of ethical and legal issues related to conducting this type of program. This section addresses some of the most common issues you may encounter. It is essential that you be informed about your own specific school and district guidelines and state laws.

Confidentiality

When conducting ADAPT, confidentiality is an issue of utmost importance that you will need to address. Students have a right to know what types of information will or will not be shared by you outside the group with a third party, such as a parent or administrator. If students do not understand how confidentiality will be handled, they will not be comfortable sharing information about themselves.

To appropriately address confidentiality, you need to clearly understand how issues of confidentiality are handled in your school because rules and procedures vary across school settings. Procedures must also be in place to cover cases when confidentiality is broken—either intentionally or unintentionally. You can make confidentiality requirements part of the group rules that you establish in the first ADAPT session.

The confidentiality guidelines presented next are what work best *in general* when conducting ADAPT. If some of these guidelines are not congruent with the procedures in your school, you may wish to negotiate these issues with school administrators. Make sure you have administrative agreement regarding any deviations from the established procedures in your school well in advance of initiating the program. Make agreed-upon rules and guidelines clear to all parties involved—students, parents, school faculty, and administrators.

General confidentiality guidelines include:

1 **Keep what is said in the group confidential, with certain exceptions.** Standard exceptions include instances when a student is at risk for harming him/herself or others, or when there is a report of abuse. *Note*: You will need to determine the appropriate confidentiality and exceptions based on state laws and your particular school and district guidelines.

2 **Students should be expected to keep what is said in the group confidential.** However, you may find that students do occasionally break confidentiality. A situation in which a student intentionally breaks

ADAPT: Advancing Decision Making and Problem Solving for Teens **23**

SECTION 2.5 ETHICAL AND LEGAL ISSUES

confidentiality by gossiping about another group member with someone who isn't in the group is called "Hallway Gossip." A situation in which a student unintentionally breaks confidentiality by talking about another group member with someone who isn't in the group out of concern for that group member is called "Concern Talk." Even though the motivations for these types of confidentiality breaches may be different, they are both treated the same. Session 1 includes suggestions for addressing this issue within the context of establishing the group rules, one of which entails brainstorming with students about how to handle such breaches.

3 **Explain to students that confidentiality cannot be guaranteed 100%.** Let students know that, because of the nature of a group, confidentiality can never be guaranteed. This applies to all groups. As the facilitator, you cannot monitor the behavior of all student members. Therefore, students in a group have a responsibility to police themselves so that confidentiality is not broken. (Students may have many questions about this particular issue and their questions should be answered thoroughly in the very first ADAPT session and thereafter as they arise.)

4 **Any zero-tolerance guidelines need to be clarified in advance of sessions.** The norms and guidelines for zero-tolerance infractions vary from school to school. If your school has a zero-tolerance rule, it may mean that consequences are given to students for any behavior seen as dangerous to the school environment. Typical examples include fighting, using drugs, threatening violence to another person, and bringing a weapon to school. Zero-tolerance policies are generally put in place based on the premise that schools are safer when students receive severe consequences, such as suspension or expulsion, for certain behaviors that are considered dangerous.

Many of the same students who are in need of targeted or intensive interventions have also experienced zero-tolerance infractions. Unfortunately, the research on zero tolerance suggests that there is little evidence that enforcement of these policies makes schools safer (American Psychological Association Zero Tolerance Task Force, 2008). In fact, enforcement of these policies can cause students who are already at risk to have a less positive connection with the school because of the consequences administered.

If your school has a zero-tolerance policy, issues may arise when implementing ADAPT. Because of the nature of the topics covered in the program, students are likely to discuss behaviors that fall under zero-

24 *Section 2: Important Considerations*

tolerance guidelines. This can create problems if you feel that you have to report a student any time drug use, anger, or aggression is discussed. For this reason, discuss whether school administrators will require you to report these types of discussions before you begin the program.

You and the administration must balance the need to maintain and to break confidentiality. It is important that you work together to identify the types of zero-tolerance infractions that must be reported (for example, behaviors that would clearly cause harm to the student or to others) and those behaviors that fall in a gray area. The importance of maintaining confidentiality cannot be overemphasized. If students do not feel that what they disclose in the group is protected, they will not be comfortable and are unlikely to benefit from the group sessions. After you have come to a workable agreement with school administrators, openly discuss this issue with parents and students before beginning the group and with students thoroughly in the first session and thereafter as needed.

Mental Health Issues

ADAPT is not a mental health treatment. Some of the students targeted for the ADAPT program may have mental health issues that predate their participation. This may include prior or concurrent work with counselors, therapists, or psychiatrists for mental health issues such as depression, anxiety, substance abuse, and ADHD. Some students may also take prescribed medications for those conditions. It is important for you to be aware that students may elect to share varying levels of their past or present treatment as they relate to these conditions. There may also be situations in which you suspect a student is exhibiting signs of an undiagnosed mental health concern. If this happens, you will need to determine if referral to a mental health professional is warranted.

Be clear with students and parents that ADAPT is not designed as a treatment for any mental health condition. Hence, you may need to arrange for some students to obtain referrals, or encourage their ongoing participation in treatment for mental health issues.

Signs of a Depressive Disorder

If a student exhibits five or more of these signs during the same two-week period, a referral to a mental health professional may be warranted. These behaviors represent changes from how the student normally behaves.

- Poor concentration or difficulty remembering things
- Hard time getting things done or inability to do schoolwork
- Loss of interest in activities that used to be enjoyed; things are not fun anymore; feelings of boredom a lot of the time
- Indecisiveness or low confidence or self-esteem
- Hard time feeling good; crying a lot; others say student is moody; thinks/talks about suicide
- Hard time getting going; no energy to do anything; feeling tired most of the time
- Insomnia or sleeping too much; not being able to fall asleep or waking up in the night
- Poor appetite or overeating; changes in appetite— eating more or less than usual

Source: *Diagnostic and Statistical Manual of Mental Disorders*, Fourth Edition (American Psychiatric Association, 2000).

ADAPT: Advancing Decision Making and Problem Solving for Teens

SECTION 2.6

Connecting With Parents/Guardians

How do you effectively connect with parents/guardians?

Unfortunately, parents/guardians of at-risk students are often contacted by school personnel only when their son or daughter has committed an infraction and will receive a consequence as a result. Over time, these repeated negative interactions can limit the willingness of parents/guardians to engage with the school. The following guidelines will help you develop and maintain positive home connections. Parents/guardians can be important allies who can reinforce attendance and skill practice in the home environment.

Beginning of the Program

- *Obtain permission.* Initially, contact parents/guardians to obtain permission for their son or daughter to participate in ADAPT. Follow your school and district guidelines for obtaining permission. Use your standard school permission form or modify Reproducible A-2 on the CD to meet your state and school requirements.

- *Establish positive rapport.* This is a good time for you to begin establishing positive connections with the parents/guardians of students who participate in ADAPT. Start by letting them know the value of the program and how their child can benefit.

It is important to engage parents/guardians in a positive manner from the very beginning of the program. Consider the following hypothetical situation in which a facilitator contacts a parent regarding his son's participation in ADAPT:

I know Mark has been struggling with making good choices lately. The reason I'm calling is because Mark has the opportunity to participate in a group program called ADAPT. The goals of this program are to help students improve their problem-solving and decision-making skills. We know that improving these skills helps teens make better choices and prevents them from engaging in behaviors that will cause them problems. I think Mark would be a good fit for the program. What do you think about this?

The facilitator in this scenario is making an effort to explain to the parent that his son has an opportunity to participate in a program that will teach him skills he can use to address issues that have been challenging for him and to hopefully prevent future problem behavior; this is a strength-based approach. This type of interaction encourages the parent to see his son's participation in the program as an opportunity rather than a consequence.

26   *Section 2: Important Considerations*

Contrast the scenario described above with the following:

I know Mark has been making bad decisions lately. He was caught smelling of alcohol last week in class, and his grades and attendance are going downhill. He is headed for big problems if he doesn't straighten things out. Because he has been having so many problems, I recommend that he participate in a program called ADAPT that is for kids like him. I know he has participated in other programs before, but this is another one he can try. Let's give this a try. What do you think?

The facilitator's approach in this scenario focuses on Mark's deficits and implies that participation in ADAPT is a negative consequence for his problem behaviors. This deficit- or consequence-based approach presents ADAPT as a punishment rather than as an opportunity for improvement.

The first scenario is also more likely to help you achieve the goal of "enrolling" the parent/guardian as a supportive ally of the program.

- *Provide a general overview of the session topics, what they will cover, and how issues of confidentiality will be handled.* Everyone—you, the students, and their parents/guardians—should be on the same page regarding what participation in the program entails. Present participation in the program as an opportunity to build important skills rather than as a consequence for prior problem behavior. Reproducible A-3 provides an overview of the ADAPT program. You can customize the form provided on the CD with specifics about your group.

During the Program

Maintain contact with parents/guardians during the course of the group. Ways you can keep in touch include:

- *Every third session, send brief mailings home to parents/guardians.* Include a general descriptive outline of the material to be covered during the next three sessions and blank copies of the practice sheets (take-home assignments that involve practicing skills learned). See Reproducibles A-4 through A-7 on the CD for examples you can customize.

- *Make brief phone calls to check in.* Call parents/guardians to briefly check in and encourage them to ask their son or daughter about his or her participation in ADAPT. Provide information and gentle reminders about the practice sheets. During phone calls with parents/guardians, keep in mind the confidentiality rules that you established at the beginning of the

SECTION 2.6 CONNECTING WITH PARENTS/GUARDIANS

program. Do your utmost to respect each student's sense of privacy. Only share things that are general in nature, except in those cases where there is a concern about the welfare of the student, as discussed earlier. Inform students about any contact you have with their parents/guardians so they do not feel like they are being talked about behind their backs. Positive contacts can go a long way in strengthening the support of parents/guardians for their child's participation in the program.

At Program Termination

At the end of the program, mail a satisfaction survey to parents/guardians to obtain their feedback about the program (see Reproducible A-8, Parent/Guardian Satisfaction Survey; a customizable version is provided on the CD). This type of information gathering lets parents/guardians know you are interested in any feedback they can provide. Their participation will make them

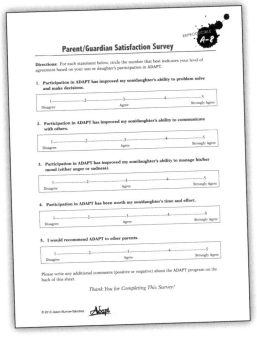

stronger advocates of the program. You can use the data to understand the perspective of parents and what you might do in the future to enhance your relationships with parents/guardians and strengthen your ADAPT implementation.

If you decide to use any of the suggestions above, make sure that you inform students and parents what you plan to do from the beginning of the program; doing this will help to dispel any concerns students may have about your talking to their parents. It is also a good idea to inform students when you have talked with their parents (for example, in the next group session) so they are kept "in the loop."

28   Section 1: Overview

SECTION 2.7

Collecting Data and Evaluating Outcomes

How can you monitor progress and outcomes for the program?

Monitoring the progress and outcomes of ADAPT is important so you can evaluate the effects of the program. Information you gather can demonstrate to administrators and other school staff that the program works. Collect the types of data that are most relevant for your particular setting. Suggestions include:

1 Attendance Data
Have students sign an attendance sheet at the beginning of each session, or keep track of attendance yourself. Tracking attendance on a session-by-session basis allows you to quickly determine if it is at acceptable levels (for example, 80% or higher).

2 Practice Sheets
Each session includes an out-of-session practice sheet that is due at the next session. Collect practice sheet completion data. Keep a tally of who has completed the practice sheets at the beginning of each session. This will allow you to quickly determine if practice sheet completion rates are at acceptable levels (for example, 80% or higher).

Note: You can record attendance and practice sheet completion data using the tracking chart provided as a Microsoft Excel worksheet (see Attendance_Practice Sheet Data.xlsx on the CD). After inputting the data, you can easily transfer it to the tracking graphs to provide an easy-to-interpret visual representation of the data.

3 Satisfaction Surveys
It is increasingly important to understand how students (direct consumers) and parents and teachers (indirect consumers) view a program in the school setting. Survey data also allow program administrators to understand how a particular program is received and what components should be continued or modified. Consumer satisfaction and confidence is important. If students perceive the program to be beneficial, they are more likely to attend and participate. In addition, parents and teachers are more likely to support a program when they perceive it to be beneficial to students. These variables are important to the sustainability of the program.

Note: Parent/Guardian (Reproducible A-8), Student (Reproducible A-9), and Teacher (Reproducible A-10) Satisfaction Surveys are included on the CD in both PDF and Microsoft Word formats so that you can easily modify them to fit the needs of your school setting. The surveys should be

ADAPT: Advancing Decision Making and Problem Solving for Teens

SECTION 2.7 COLLECTING DATA AND EVALUATING OUTCOMES

administered immediately after the program has been completed. Each survey is scaled so that higher scores indicate higher agreement. You can examine each survey individually or group them by respondent category (parent/guardian, teacher, and student). Grouping them by respondent category can be very helpful in understanding how a particular group viewed the program. In the example below (Table 1-2), the scores of individual items have been entered into a spreadsheet for each parent, and the average rating for each item is displayed in the last column. You can see from question #1 that, on average, parents rated improvement in their son or daughter's ability to problem solve and make decisions based on their participation in the program as a "4." The rating of 4 on a scale of 1–5 (1=disagree, 5=strongly agree) indicates high agreement. You can also see, based on an average rating of "5" for question #5, that parents, on average, strongly agreed that they would recommend this program to other parents.

Table 1-2

Sample results from Parent/Guardian ADAPT Satisfaction Survey

Respondent Group	Parent 1	Parent 2	Parent 3	Parent 4	Parent 5	Average Rating
Question #1	4	4	4	4	5	4
Question #2	5	3	4	2	5	4
Question #3	3	4	5	3	3	4
Question #4	4	5	5	5	4	5
Question #5	4	5	5	5	4	5

4 **Outcome Measures**
A range of outcome measures exist that you can also use for ADAPT because of the broad content areas that the program covers.

Generally, outcome measures should be brief self-report instruments that you give to students prior to the beginning of the program as a pre-test or baseline indicator of the behavior being measured. The same measure should then be administered again immediately following completion of the program. Scores from both measures are then compared to determine if any change has occurred in the anticipated direction. Measures for some of the areas indicated are in the public domain and can therefore be used free of charge. Other measures will need to be obtained through their respective author(s) or publisher, and there may be a charge for their use.

Examples of direct outcome areas to measure:

- Problem solving
- Decision making
- Depressive symptoms
- Self-esteem
- Drug use
- Delinquency
- Social support

Examples of indirect outcome areas to measure:

- School attendance
- Grade point average
- Office discipline referrals

The particular types of outcomes measured will depend on the type of information most relevant to your school setting. For example, in some schools it may be more relevant to know if drug use or delinquency decreased based on participation in the program, whereas in other schools it may more important to understand the effects the program has had on office discipline referrals or school attendance.

HOW SESSIONS WORK

SECTION 3

Section 3.1 — Session Structure

How are ADAPT sessions structured?

For ease of use, each session guide follows a recognizable pattern.

Opener

- **Session Goals**
  At a glance, you can determine how your students will benefit from the individual session.

- **Session Preparation**
  This easy-to-reference guide will get you ready for your session.

- **Materials**
  Follow the bullets so you have all the needed materials ready for your session. All reproducible materials are provided on the CD.

- **About This Session**
  The right column provides a short narrative summary of the session along with important notes.

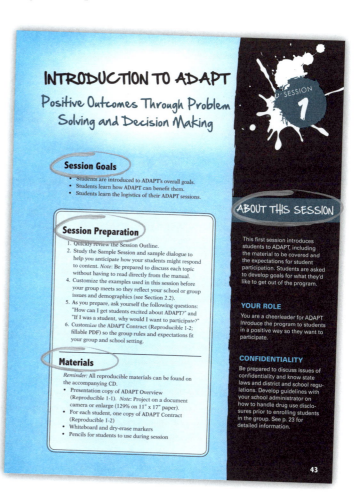

33

SECTION 3.1 SESSION STRUCTURE

Session Outline

The three- to four-page Session Outline provides a brief, unscripted plan for the session. Use this for a quick preview/review of session activities and as a quick reference guide during the session.

- *Beginning the Session*
  After a warm welcome, students introduce themselves in Session 1. Following Session 1, each session begins with students sharing and discussing completed practice sheets (assignments).

- *Presenting the Topic and Practicing Skills*
  The body of each session focuses on the presentation of a new skill and practicing the skill through the use of graphic organizers, scenarios, application to student examples, and role-plays. The two-page session plan uses large, easy-to-follow numbers to guide you through the session.

- *Ending the Session*
  Each session ends with the assignment of an out-of-session practice sheet. (See Section 3.2 for more information.)

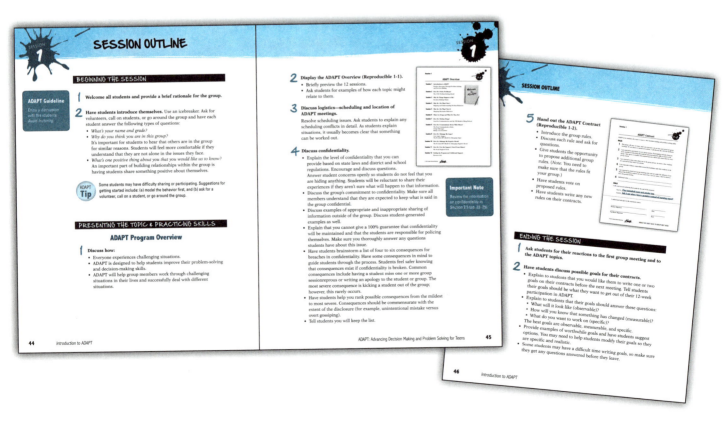

34 Section 3: How Sessions Work

Sample Session

This comprehensive guide follows the Session Outline and provides an in-depth look at how a session might actually sound. This partially scripted study guide presents facilitators with an example of how students might respond to activities. By reading the guide, you can anticipate your own students' interactions with the materials and develop a strong vision of how to guide your group through the strategies provided. The first time you run an ADAPT group, we strongly recommend studying the Sample Session in advance of your meetings.

Do you need to cover all the material in each session?

Each of the 12 sessions is designed to stand on its own and be delivered separately, but fit into the program as a whole.

In general, the material presented in each session is meant to be covered in a single session. However, the program is designed so that material not covered in one session can be covered in the next. Sessions link together naturally through review of the practice sheet assigned in the previous session.

Most sessions include multiple activities, so you may need to make decisions about what material to cover based on time constraints. As you review the Facilitator's Study Guide, you may wish to determine what you might leave out if the group is highly engaged and activities take longer than anticipated.

As you become more experienced and more fluent in delivering the lessons, some activities will take less time.

Combining Sessions 4 and 5

Material in Sessions 4 and 5 builds on prior sessions (problem solving, decision making) but is typically more difficult for students to comprehend. In particular, some students will have more difficulty understanding the conceptual and practical aspects of mapping behaviors. Sessions 4 and 5 are designed to give students a broader understanding of how triggers (antecedents), behaviors, and consequences are related. Session 4 details mapping to understand negative behaviors, and Session 5 details mapping for alternative positive behaviors. You can present the sessions separately as they appear in the manual or combine the material across both sessions (recommended). Also note that the concepts underlying mapping are similar to those underlying Functional Assessment (FA). It is assumed that many school personnel will have prior experience with FAs and, thus, additional knowledge to draw from when illustrating and teaching the concepts and skills covered in these sessions.

ADAPT: Advancing Decision Making and Problem Solving for Teens   **35**

SECTION 3.2

Practice Sheets

What are practice sheets and how are they used?

Practice sheets ("homework") are designed to provide students with opportunities to practice skills between group sessions. At the end of every session, each student receives a practice sheet that targets the specific topic and skills learned during that session. Students are asked to practice the specific skill(s), record their progress, and bring their completed practice sheets to the next group session and share their progress with the rest of the group.

Why are practice sheets important?

Practice sheets serve several purposes. First, by assigning practice sheets, you let students know that you expect them to practice skills outside of the group session. From a learning perspective, this helps students generalize the skills to their daily lives. Second, research suggests that practicing skills outside of an intervention program typically produces better results than practicing the skills only during the program. Third, you can use practice sheets to assess skill strengths and weaknesses for each student. Finally, practice sheets help structure group sessions by serving as a recurrent activity that links one session with the next.

Why is the term "practice sheet" used instead of "homework"?

The term *practice sheet* is intentionally used because at-risk students frequently develop negative connotations for the term *homework*. To these students, homework may remind them of failure or of something they do poorly. Students who have low self-efficacy for completing homework assignments are less likely to attempt (and complete) the assignment.

On the other hand, practice sheets represent "doable" skills that all students can practice between sessions. These assignments have no right or wrong answers. To successfully complete a practice sheet, students need only make an effort to practice the skills and then report back on their progress. Although you will have students with different learning abilities, you should expect that all students can acquire the skills with continued practice. If you suspect that a student has poor reading or writing skills that interfere with comprehension and completion of practice sheets, you should discuss this issue with the student privately and determine a plan for overcoming this obstacle (in addition to making sure the student is connected with reading resources in your

---

Generalization

One important purpose of the practice sheets is to help students generalize the skills learned in ADAPT to natural settings outside of the group environment. The more students practice skills, the more natural and second nature they will become. This increases the likelihood that students will continue to use their newly learned skills after the group has ended and be able to effect a positive and permanent change in the way they deal with difficult situations.

---

36   *Section 3: How Sessions Work*

school). Suggestions include asking the student to meet for few minutes before or after group so you can review the practice sheet with him or her, or being available for a few minutes between weekly sessions to review the practice sheet with the student.

Do students always return their practice sheets?

Just like homework, students may not always turn in their practice sheets. Increasing the number of students who return their practice sheets should be a goal that you help the group work on as the program proceeds. Return rates will be lowest during the first few group sessions and then gradually increase over the course of the program. Let students know that to receive credit for a completed practice sheet, they must meet two requirements: 1) their practice sheet must be complete, and 2) their practice sheet must be returned at the beginning of the appropriate session. If a student completes his or her practice sheet but forgets to bring it to the group session, it is not considered a completed practice sheet.

How can you encourage students to complete their practice sheets?

You can use any or all of the strategies below to increase the rate of practice sheet completion. Some groups will have a high rate of practice sheet return while others will have an extremely low rate of return. Most groups will fall somewhere in the middle. Do not feel limited to the strategies suggested here.

- *From the first session onward, state and then reinforce the expectation that each student will complete and return his or her practice sheet.* This expectation is part of the group contract covered during the first session.

- *Work with students to problem solve and eliminate obstacles that prevent them from completing their practice sheets,* especially during the first few sessions as the norm for practice sheet completion is being established.

- *At the beginning of each session, praise the students who completed their practice sheets.* Ask the remaining students what prevented them from completing their practice sheets, and then ask the group to problem solve how to overcome those obstacles. Focus the discussion on the positive behavior you want to increase (practice sheet completion) rather than on

ADAPT: Advancing Decision Making and Problem Solving for Teens   **37**

SECTION 3.2 **PRACTICE SHEETS**

the problem behavior (forgetting the practice sheet). Your goal is to help the students determine how they can successfully return practice sheets to group sessions.

- *If a student returns a blank practice sheet at the beginning of the session, don't let him or her off the hook.* Instead, tell the student that he or she will need to complete the practice sheet right now as the group reviews the other practice sheets that were turned in. Also help the student problem solve ways to complete practice sheets in the future.

- *Reinforce the students who completed their practice sheets through a random drawing at the beginning of each session.* Put the names of the students who completed their practice sheets into a hat at the beginning of the session. Then pick one name at random and give that student a small reinforcer appropriate to the setting.

- *Tell students that you will keep a tally of how many in the group complete their practice sheets each week.* Whenever the group achieves a 75% or higher (choose a realistic percentage for your particular group) rate of return, reward the group with a small reinforcer. When the group achieves its goal, increase the goal slightly to continue challenging the students. If the group does not achieve its goal, help the group problem solve ways to reach their goal. Make sure the tally or percentage is posted somewhere highly visible, such as a whiteboard, to remind students of the goal and their accomplishments. This strategy utilizes the natural peer pressure found in groups to provide extra incentive for students to complete their practice sheets, especially those students who are not regularly completing their practice sheets and who will feel pressure to not let the group down.

- *If a student arrives to a session early with an incomplete practice sheet, you can allow him or her to use the extra time to complete it.* Use this strategy at your own discretion because it may work well for some students but not others. Don't use this strategy consistently with any single student, but only as a last-minute solution. Consistently using this strategy with a particular student may send the message that completing the practice sheet at the beginning of a session rather than between sessions is acceptable. If you use this strategy, discuss ways the student can overcome the obstacles that prevented him or her from completing the practice sheet before the session.

- *Implement your own creative strategies to improve the rate of practice sheet completion in your groups.* As you do so, keep in mind that your goal should be to increase and reward desired behaviors (completing practice sheets) rather than to punish undesired behaviors (forgetting practice sheets).

38   *Section 3: How Sessions Work*

Group Development Across Sessions

SECTION
3.3

What developmental stages do groups typically go through?

All groups develop over time, with most groups progressing through several general stages. Knowing what these stages are will help you understand some of the typical student behaviors you can expect to see at various points in the program (Burrow-Sánchez & Hawken, 2007; Corey & Corey, 2006).

1 Opening Stage

This stage occurs in the first couple of group sessions. During this stage, students will want to know the purpose and structure of the group, how issues of confidentiality will be handled, and how they will benefit from the group. Specifically, they will want to know, "What's in it for me?" During this stage, you will feel like you are doing more work than the students because you will be setting the foundation for the group. Students will be less likely to spontaneously participate during the early part of this stage, but their participation will increase as their understanding of the group norms grow.

2 Transition Stage

The transition stage usually occurs during the third and fourth session. After the foundation has been laid in the opening stage, students will want to move on to the work they will be expected to do in the group. During the transition stage, issues of confidentiality and the value of the group sessions are resolved.

If important issues aren't resolved during the transition stage, the group can get stalled. Indications of unresolved issues include lack of participation, expressions of disinterest or discomfort, and verbal or nonverbal challenges. It's important to address any issues that you think are keeping the group "stuck" in this stage because the group will not become productive until you do so.

3 Working Stage

The working stage begins after the group is done transitioning and students are comfortable in the group. During this stage, you will encounter fewer challenges and less resistance from students. You will be able to focus more on working through the material in **ADAPT** rather than on dealing with initial group setup issues. Students will be more open to engaging in and participating in the material. The specific behaviors you will see include the following:

ADAPT: Advancing Decision Making and Problem Solving for Teens   **39**

SECTION 3.3 GROUP DEVELOPMENT ACROSS SESSIONS

- Students engage in more in-depth discussions.
- Students role-play to practice new skills.
- Students express personal challenges or difficulties.
- Students offer other group members feedback and support.

Students will also be more likely to express ownership for the group at this stage.

4 Termination Stage

The termination stage should begin three sessions before the end of the program. Initiate discussions about the program ending three sessions before it occurs so students can move productively toward ending. Don't assume that students will remember the established ending date. Reasons for discussing the program's ending include:

- Prompting students to participate fully before the program ends.
- Helping students understand that they still have time to discuss skills and ask questions.
- Encouraging discussion about school and community options for additional support after the program ends.

SESSION PLANS

SECTION 4

Each session plan consists of two parts—the Session Outline and a Sample Session that includes dialogue. The Sample Session helps you anticipate and visualize how your sessions might evolve. This will enhance your ability to keep your sessions targeted yet customized to your group.

The sample scripts in the Sample Session should not be read to students but are provided to help you anticipate how to respond to student questions and comments. Use your own words to guide the session.

The session plans are:

Session 1: Introduction to ADAPT. Positive Outcomes Through Problem Solving and Decision Making

Session 2: How Do I Solve Problems? The 4-Ws Problem-Solving Model

Session 3: Why Do Things Happen to Me? Decision-Making Chains

Session 4: Why Do I Do That? Part I. Mapping and Understanding Problem Behaviors

Session 5: Why Do I Do That? Part II. Mapping Alternative Behaviors

Session 6: What Are Drugs and What Do They Do?

Session 7: How Do I Refuse Drugs? Triggers, Communication, Reasons

Session 8: How Do I Communicate Better With Others? Assertive Communication Skills

Session 9: How Do I Manage My Anger?

Session 10: How Do I Manage My Negative Mood?

Session 11: How Do I Get the Support I Need From Others?

Session 12: Ending the Program and Additional Support

INTRODUCTION TO ADAPT
Positive Outcomes Through Problem Solving and Decision Making

SESSION 1

Session Goals

- Students are introduced to ADAPT's overall goals.
- Students learn how ADAPT can benefit them.
- Students learn the logistics of their ADAPT sessions.

Session Preparation

1. Quickly review the Session Outline.
2. Study the Sample Session and sample dialogue to help you anticipate how your students might respond to content. *Note*: Be prepared to discuss each topic without having to read directly from the manual.
4. Customize the examples used in this session before your group meets so they reflect your school or group issues and demographics (see Section 2.2).
5. As you prepare, ask yourself the following questions: "How can I get students excited about ADAPT?" and "If I was a student, why would I want to participate?"
6. Customize the ADAPT Contract (Reproducible 1-2; fillable PDF) so the group rules and expectations fit your group and school setting.

Materials

Reminder: All reproducible materials can be found on the accompanying CD.
- Presentation copy of ADAPT Overview (Reproducible 1-1). *Note*: Project on a document camera or enlarge (129% on 11" x 17" paper).
- For each student, one copy of ADAPT Contract (Reproducible 1-2)
- Whiteboard and dry-erase markers
- Pencils for students to use during session

ABOUT THIS SESSION

This first session introduces students to ADAPT, including the material to be covered and the expectations for student participation. Students are asked to develop goals for what they'd like to get out of the program.

YOUR ROLE

You are a cheerleader for ADAPT. Inroduce the program to students in a positive way so they want to participate.

CONFIDENTIALITY

Be prepared to discuss issues of confidentiality and know state laws and district and school regulations. Develop guidelines with your school administrator on how to handle drug use disclosures prior to enrolling students in the group. See p. 23 for detailed information.

SESSION OUTLINE

SESSION 1

BEGINNING THE SESSION

> **ADAPT Guideline**
>
> Enjoy a *discussion* with the students. Avoid *lecturing*.

1 Welcome all students and provide a brief rationale for the group.

2 **Have students introduce themselves.** Use an icebreaker. Ask for volunteers, call on students, or go around the group and have each student answer the following types of questions:

- *What's your name and grade?*
- *Why do you think you are in this group?*
  It's important for students to hear that others are in the group for similar reasons. Students will feel more comfortable if they understand that they are not alone in the issues they face.
- *What's one positive thing about you that you would like us to know?*
  An important part of building relationships within the group is having students share something positive about themselves.

Some students may have difficulty sharing or participating. Suggestions for getting started include: (a) model the behavior first, and (b) ask for a volunteer, call on a student, or go around the group.

PRESENTING THE TOPIC & PRACTICING SKILLS

ADAPT Program Overview

1 **Discuss how:**

- Everyone experiences challenging situations.
- ADAPT is designed to help students improve their problem-solving and decision-making skills.
- ADAPT will help group members work through challenging situations in their lives and successfully deal with different situations.

Introduction to ADAPT

2 **Display the ADAPT Overview (Reproducible 1-1).**
- Briefly preview the 12 sessions.
- Ask students for examples of how each topic might relate to them.

3 **Discuss logistics—scheduling and location of ADAPT meetings.**

Resolve scheduling issues. Ask students to explain any scheduling conflicts in detail. As students explain situations, it usually becomes clear that something can be worked out.

4 **Discuss confidentiality.**
- Explain the level of confidentiality that you can provide based on state laws and district and school regulations. Encourage and discuss questions. Answer student concerns openly so students do not feel that you are hiding anything. Students will be reluctant to share their experiences if they aren't sure what will happen to that information.
- Discuss the group's commitment to confidentiality. Make sure all members understand that they are expected to keep what is said in the group confidential.
- Discuss examples of appropriate and inappropriate sharing of information outside of the group. Discuss student-generated examples as well.
- Explain that you cannot give a 100% guarantee that confidentiality will be maintained and that the students are responsible for policing themselves. Make sure you thoroughly answer any questions students have about this issue.
- Have students brainstorm a list of four to six consequences for breaches in confidentiality. Have some consequences in mind to guide students through the process. Students feel safer knowing that consequences exist if confidentiality is broken. Common consequences include having a student miss one or more group sessionreprous or writing an apology to the student or group. The most severe consequence is kicking a student out of the group; however, this rarely occurs.
- Have students help you rank possible consequences from the mildest to most severe. Consequences should be commensurate with the extent of the disclosure (for example, unintentional mistake versus overt gossiping).
- Tell students you will keep the list.

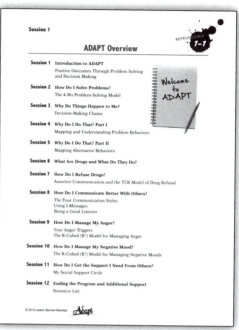

Important Note

Review the information on confidentiality in Section 2.5 (pp. 23–25).

ADAPT: Advancing Decision Making and Problem Solving for Teens   45

SESSION OUTLINE

5 **Hand out the ADAPT Contract (Reproducible 1-2).**

- Introduce the group rules.
- Discuss each rule and ask for questions.
- Give students the opportunity to propose additional group rules. (*Note:* You need to make sure that the rules fit your group.)
- Have students vote on proposed rules.
- Have students write any new rules on their contracts.

ENDING THE SESSION

1 **Ask students for their reactions to the first group meeting and to the ADAPT topics.**

2 **Have students discuss possible goals for their contracts.**

- Explain to students that you would like them to write one or two goals on their contracts before the next meeting. Tell students their goals should be what they want to get out of their 12-week participation in ADAPT.
- Explain to students that their goals should answer these questions:
    - What will it look like (observable)?
    - How will you know that something has changed (measurable)?
    - What do you want to work on (specific)?

  The best goals are observable, measurable, and specific.
- Provide examples of worthwhile goals and have students suggest options. You may need to help students modify their goals so they are specific and realistic.
- Some students may have a difficult time writing goals, so make sure they get any questions answered before they leave.

Introduction to ADAPT

SAMPLE SESSION

This sample session includes examples of dialogue to help you anticipate and visualize how your sessions might evolve. This will enhance your ability to keep your sessions targeted yet customized to your group.

The sample scripts should not be read to students but are provided to help you anticipate how to respond to student questions and comments. Use your own words to guide the session.

BEGINNING THE SESSION

1. Welcome all students and provide a brief rationale for the group.

Welcome to the group! My name is Mr. Sánchez, and I will be leading the group for the next 12 weeks. I am a school counselor and as part of my job, I work with small groups of high school students.

We'll have a chance to get to know everyone in a few minutes, but first I want to explain more about this group. We are going to meet 12 times over the next 3 months to work on improving important skills that we use every day. These skills are problem solving and decision making. Improving these skills will help you deal with challenging situations and problems that create stress for you.

Each week we'll discuss a slightly different topic and ways to improve our problem solving and decision making in that area. It is important that each of you find ways to relate what you learn in the program to what's going on in your own lives. This will make the material more real and interesting for you. For example, we will talk about things like how to improve your problem-solving skills, what to do when your mood is down, how to deal with others when you are angry, and how to get support from others.

One of my goals is to help each of you find ways to make this group useful, so we'll try to apply the skills to situations you face every day.

2. Have students introduce themselves. Use an icebreaker. Ask for volunteers, call on students, or go around the group and have each student answer the following types of questions:

- *What's your name and grade?*
- *Why do you think you are in this group?*
  It's important for students to hear that others are in the group for similar reasons. Students will feel more comfortable if they understand that they are not alone in the issues they face.
- *What's one positive thing about you that you would like us to know?*
  An important part of building relationships within the group is having students share something positive about themselves.

Let's start getting to know each other. Tell us your name and grade.
My name is Ryan and I'm a sophomore.

ADAPT: Advancing Decision Making and Problem Solving for Teens   47

SAMPLE SESSION

Ryan, why do you think you are in this group? I'm here because my school counselor told me to come—because of some problems I had.

*OK, Ryan. What's something positive you'd like us to know about you?
Well, I guess I'm good at skateboarding.*

Some students may have difficulty sharing, and/or you may experience a lack of participation from the group. Suggestions for getting the activity started include:

a. Model the behavior first.

   *I'm going to have you introduce yourselves, but first I'll introduce myself again so you can see how it works.
   My name is Mr. Sánchez and I am a school counselor.
   I am in the group because I like working with adolescents.
   One positive thing about me is that I am able to make friends easily.*

b. Ask for a volunteer, call on a student, or go around the group.

   Volunteers. If you ask for volunteers to introduce themselves, you may need to wait awhile. If you are not comfortable with silence, this may not be the best option; however, if you wait long enough, someone is likely to volunteer. The silence may initially feel uncomfortable for you and others in the group.

   Ask a specific student to go first. This works best if you know ahead of time which students are socially adept and likely to comply with your request. After the student finishes, ask that student to select the next student.

PRESENTING THE TOPIC & PRACTICING SKILLS

ADAPT Program Overview

1 **Discuss how:**

- Everyone experiences challenging situations.

  Everyone periodically faces a challenging situation. It sounds like many of you are here for similar reasons. For example, Jamal and Maria indicated they were here because they had gotten angry with adults in the school; Ryan said he had some similar problems.

- ADAPT is designed to help students improve their problem-solving and decision-making skills.

  Each time we meet, we will discuss a topic that helps you improve skills in different areas of your life.

Introduction to ADAPT

SESSION 1

- **ADAPT** will help students work through challenging situations in their lives and successfully deal with different situations.

  As I briefly preview these topics, I want you to think about how you can apply them to situations you face in your daily lives. If you learn how to apply the ADAPT strategies in your own life, it will make your participation in our group worth your time.

2 Display the ADAPT Overview (Reproducible 1-1).

- Briefly preview the 12 sessions and ask students how each topic might relate to them.

  Point to each session on the overview.

  Session 1 is an Introduction to ADAPT. Our goal for today is to learn more about ADAPT, how the program works, and what will be expected of you over the next 12 weeks.

  Session 2 is How Do I Solve Problems? We'll work on this topic next week. We'll discuss how to solve problems more effectively. Solving problems is sometimes hard for me, so this session is one that I find very useful.

  Session 3 is Why Do Things Happen to Me? Do you ever wonder why bad things happen to you? Angie? Yeah. Things just happen. It's like I have a curse on me or something.

  Who else feels that way? I'm not surprised to see you nodding your heads. We all feel that life isn't fair sometimes. It's important to understand how bad things happen and how you can prevent them from happening.

  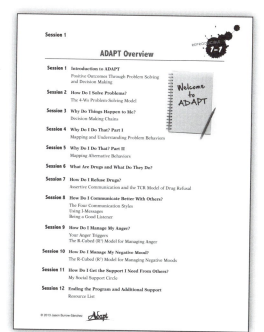

  In Session 3, you will learn how to use a Decision-Making Chain. It will help you understand how "bad things" happen and how you can take control of situations.

  Sessions 4 and 5 are Why Do I Do That? Part 1 and Part 2. In these sessions, we'll talk about understanding why you do certain things even though they can lead to bad outcomes. Can you relate to this? Megan? Yeah, sometimes I do things even though I know it probably won't turn out well.

  You are making great connections here. We'll work on Problem-Solving Maps. They will help you understand why you do things and choose behaviors that lead to better outcomes.

  Session 6 is What Are Drugs and What Do They Do? In this session, we'll talk about what drugs are and what they do. Accurate information about drugs and what they do to a person is important so you can make good decisions. You may think that you know a lot about drugs, but much of the information out there is not accurate. If you have bad information, do you think you can you make good decisions? Who has questions about drugs? Maria? Yes, I have a lot of questions, and I'm not always sure what to believe.

ADAPT: Advancing Decision Making and Problem Solving for Teens 49

SESSION 1

SAMPLE SESSION

We all have questions, and this will be a good opportunity to get them answered.

Session 7 is How Do I Refuse Drugs? Refusing drugs can be hard depending on the situation—like who is offering the drugs and where you are. Will, do you think refusing drugs can be difficult to do? *Yeah, it can be hard for me, but it doesn't seem as hard for others.*

You aren't alone. Many teens find it hard, so we'll discuss ways to effectively refuse drugs.

Session 8 is How Do I Communicate Better With Others? Jamal, do you ever feel like people don't hear you? *Yeah—all the time.*

OK, then. Good communication can help you get your needs met. This session will help you all with that skill.

Session 9 is How Do I Manage My Anger? Do you ever feel angry? I see heads nodding.

Some of us have shorter fuses than others. I tend to not get very angry, so when I do, I'm not sure how to handle it. This session is great because everyone feels angry once in a while. So we will discuss ways to effectively manage anger.

Session 10 is How Do I Manage My Negative Mood? I'm sure most of you have felt low or depressed at one time or another. Megan, do you ever feel low? *Yes.*

It's kind of a fact of life, so it's important to know how to manage moods so they don't get the best of you.

Session 11 is How Do I Get the Support I Need From Others? All of us need support from other people in our lives, and this is normal. In fact, I don't know of anyone who can solve every situation on his or her own. It can be really helpful to obtain support from others when you are facing challenging situations, especially ones you haven't dealt with before. Support can come in the form of advice, suggestions, or someone just to listen to you.

Maria, have you ever asked another person for support? *Yes.*
Did they support you in the way you needed? *Mostly, I guess, but not totally.*

One of the things we will learn in Session 11 is how to ask for the type of support we need.

Then in our final session, Session 12, Ending the Program and Additional Support, we'll review what we've learned and how you can keep getting support.

Any thoughts? What do you think about these topics? Have you discussed these things in classes or other programs?

3 Discuss logistics—scheduling and location of ADAPT meetings.

Now we are going to talk about how the group will run over the next 12 weeks. We'll meet in this room every Tuesday for the next 12 weeks from 3 to 4 pm.

- Resolve scheduling issues. Ask students to explain any scheduling conflicts in detail. As students explain situations, it usually becomes clear that something can be worked out.

  Does anyone have any schedule conflicts? Will?
  Sometimes I'm in detention then.

  Tell me more about what that means.
  Well, if I get detention, that's when it usually is.

  OK. How often have you had detention in the past month? Just once.

  Well, first it's better if you don't receive detention, but you probably already know that. If you do get detention, let me know and we'll talk to your teacher about the possibility of serving detention at an alternative time so that you don't miss group. The most important thing is for you to communicate with me about what is going on ahead of time. That will give us time to deal with it. Does that sound OK to you? Yeah, I can do that.

 Discuss confidentiality.

- Explain the level of confidentiality that you can provide based on your state laws and district and school regulations.

  I want to spend some time discussing the issue of confidentiality, or privacy. You may wonder if any of the information you share in this group will be shared with others—your parents, teachers, the principal, school counselor, and so on. In general, the answer is "no," but there are some exceptions that I will explain.

  The information you share in this group will not be shared with anyone outside this group unless you share information that leads me to believe that you are at serious risk of hurting yourself or someone else. Another exception is if you share information that leads me to believe you are being abused or abusing someone else.

  For example, if you share information about not liking one of your teachers, that information will not be shared with anyone outside the group. However, if you tell us that you are thinking of hurting yourself or that you are having suicidal thoughts, I would need to share that information with others outside the group who can help. I would first hope to talk with you about the situation and then talk with you about sharing this information with others.

  One final time that I will share information with others is if you and your parent give me permission to provide information to another professional, such as a counselor or doctor, for some specific reason.

- Encourage and discuss questions. Answer questions openly so students do not feel that you are hiding anything. Students will be reluctant to share their experiences if they aren't sure what will happen to that information.

> **Important Note**
>
> Review the information on confidentiality in Section 2.5 (pp. 23–25).

SESSION 1

SAMPLE SESSION

Before we go further, what questions do you have about what I just said?
I was wondering what would happen if someone told the group he was using a drug like marijuana or heroin, or something like that.

That is a good question, and I'm sure you are not the only one in the group who may have been wondering about this. Remember when I discussed your participation in the group with you and your mom? Yeah, I remember.

I said that if drug use is disclosed, we take it on a case-by-case basis and consider all the factors involved. My main goal is to maintain your privacy, if possible, even in relation to drug use. I know that you won't feel comfortable in the group if you're worried about what will be said outside of the group. So it's important that we talk about these issues now.

From my experience, it becomes tricky if the drug use is related to one of the exceptions we discussed, such as harming yourself or others, but again, my goal is to maintain your privacy to the extent I am able.

Let's say someone discloses that he or she is using drugs and also selling them at school. This situation is quite different than someone who smoked marijuana at a party over the weekend. In the first situation, the person is clearly committing a crime and has the potential to hurt others in the process. In the second situation, the action has already taken place and the person is not now at serious risk of hurting himself or someone else. In the first situation, I would have no choice but to disclose it to others. In the second situation, I would try to maintain the person's privacy, if possible.

Now, what if the person is using heroin? As we will learn, heroin has a powerful, physically addictive property that can put the person at risk. Also, heroin is typically administered with a needle, so it can also put the person at risk for diseases such as HIV/AIDS. In this situation, I would need to break confidentiality.

Regardless of the situation, one of the things I can agree to do is talk with you about it first if I feel that I may need to break confidentiality. In some cases, I may just need more information from you in order to understand the situation and decide whether I will have to break confidentiality. I also want you to understand that, regardless of what I ultimately do regarding confidentiality, my overarching goal is to make sure you and others are safe.

- Discuss the group's commitment to confidentiality. Make sure all members understand that they are expected to keep what is said in the group confidential

  I just talked about what I will do with information shared in this group, but I can't control what each of you does with that information. It's important for each of you to make a commitment to keep the information shared by other students in this group confidential, or private.

  It will be your choice to share your own personal experiences in this group with others outside of the group—as long as you don't share what other students in

52   *Introduction to ADAPT*

the group have said. This may seem a little tricky or unclear, so let's think and talk about what is OK.

- Discuss examples of appropriate and inappropriate sharing of information outside of the group. Discuss student-generated examples as well.

Imagine this. You've had a good experience in the group that you want to share with a best friend who isn't in the group. You might say something like, "I told the group about the time that Mom and I had that huge argument and I hit the gas instead of the brake and drove into the garage door. The others in the group kind of snickered. It is kind of funny. But they also said they've had big arguments with their parents, too. Anyway, I got some good ideas about what to do the next time Mom and I get into an argument."

What do you think? Is that example OK? Megan? Yes.

Why is it OK? The person is just talking about what happened to her. She isn't saying what happened to someone else.

That's right. The group member is sharing about herself and did not share information about anyone else in the group.

Here's another example. Let's say one of our group members is in the hallway talking with another student who isn't in the group. Our group member says, "You know what Reggie said in the group? He said that his parents are so strict that he has to call them every half hour when he's out. He has to check in with them. Can you believe that? Man, I'm glad my parents don't do that to me!"

What do you think? Was that an OK thing to share with others who aren't in the group? You are shaking your heads "no." Why would that be wrong to share? Maria? It wouldn't be cool. If I shared something like that, I would not want the world to know. It would sound dumb.

Maria, you are right. Whether dumb or not, that example would be betraying our confidentiality rule by talking about what someone else shared. It's about Reggie, not about the person who was talking.

- Explain that you cannot give a 100% guarantee that confidentiality will be maintained and that the students are responsible for policing themselves. Make sure you thoroughly answer any questions students have about this issue.

I think it's important for you to know that I cannot guarantee 100% that confidentiality or privacy will be maintained. In other words, I can't personally guarantee that what you share in the group will not be shared by another member outside the group. Because of this, each of you has a responsibility to police yourself and respect the privacy of others. Confidentiality is up to you. It is important that you commit to not sharing what others say here outside the group. What questions do you have about this?

ADAPT: Advancing Decision Making and Problem Solving for Teens

SESSION 1

SAMPLE SESSION

- Have students brainstorm a list of four to six consequences for breaches in confidentiality. Have some consequences in mind to guide students through the process. Students feel safer knowing that consequences exist if confidentiality is broken. Common consequences include having a student miss one or more group sessions or writing an apology to the student or group. The most severe consequence is kicking a student out of the group; however, this rarely occurs.

By being part of the group, you all make a commitment to respect the privacy of everyone in the group. You can do this by keeping what's said in the group private. However, if confidentiality is broken, we need to know what the consequence should be. I'd like you to help me generate a list of possible consequences . . .

- Have students help you rank possible consequences from the mildest to the most severe. Consequences should be commensurate with the extent of the disclosure (for example, unintentional mistake versus overt gossiping).

We have a pretty good list. Let's rank them from the mildest to the most severe. The smallest consequence can be what happens the first time confidentiality is broken or if the breach is accidental.

Does everybody agree to this list?

Try to obtain consensus. If you cannot, find out why and rework your list until everyone agrees.

- Tell students you will keep the list.

5 **Hand out the ADAPT Contract (Reproducible 1-2).**

- Introduce the group rules on the contract. Your basic rules (for example, on-time, respectful) should be in the contract. These rules should be nonnegotiable and applicable to you as well.

I am passing out a group contract with rules on it. The rules I consider to be nonnegotiable and expect everyone—including myself—to follow are listed on the contract. There's also space for additional rules that you can help me with. First, I'd like to go through the basic expectations for the group.

Sample rules could include the following:
1) This group will meet 12 times, and I am expected to be on time and attend all group meetings. If I am absent or intend to be absent, I will discuss this with the facilitator.

2) I am expected to participate in every group session. Participation includes being an active member by discussing the material and practicing the skills we learn in the group. I also agree to complete the assigned practice sheets and return them to each group session.

54 *Introduction to ADAPT*

SESSION 1

3) I am expected to keep what others say in the group private. In return, other students are expected to keep what I say private.

4) I am expected to behave respectfully toward the facilitator and other students in the group.

5) I am expected to attend each group meeting sober and not under the influence of any drug. If the facilitator suspects for any reason that I am not sober, I may be asked to leave the group meeting.

- Discuss each rule and ask for questions.
- Give students the opportunity to propose group rules. (*Note:* Make sure that the rules fit your group.)

Does anyone think that any rules are missing or need to be added? Jamal? Maybe something about not interrupting other people who are talking.

OK. That will help to make rule #4 more clear, so let's write that down.

- Have students vote on proposed rules.
- Have students write any new rules on their contracts.

ENDING THE SESSION

1 Ask students for their reactions to the first group meeting and to the ADAPT topics.

Before we end today, I want to ask what you thought about today's group and about the program in general. For example, what are some things about the program that you think will be helpful? Ryan? I've got a hot temper, so I guess it would be a good thing to learn what to do when I get mad.

Excellent, Ryan. We will definitely work on that. Megan? I have a hard time saying "no" to people, so that drug refusal thing will be good.

Megan, that is a good insight.

2 Have students discuss possible goals for their contracts.

- Explain to students that you would like them to write one or two goals on their contracts before the next meeting. Tell students their goals should be what they want to get out of their 12-week participation in ADAPT.

I'd like each of you to write down one or two goals you have. If you are going to attend 12 groups, you want to make sure your time here is worthwhile.

ADAPT: Advancing Decision Making and Problem Solving for Teens

FACILITATOR'S STUDY GUIDE

- Explain to students that their goals should answer these questions:
  - What will it look like (observable)?
  - How will you know that something has changed (measurable)?
  - What do you want to work on (specific)?

  The best goals are observable, measurable, and specific.

- Provide examples of worthwhile goals and have students suggest options. You may need to help the students modify their goals so that they are specific and realistic.

  Here are some examples of worthwhile goals.
  - *I want to manage my problems with my parents better so that we argue less.*
  - *I want to improve my grades this term.*
  - *I want to not use marijuana because it gets me in trouble.*
  - *I want to communicate better with my teachers.*
  - *I want to get along better with others.*

- Some students may have a difficult time writing goals, so make sure they get any questions answered before they leave.

  You don't need to decide on your goals right now, but I want you to take your contract with you and think about what you want for your goals. Next week, bring the sheet back and we'll discuss it. Does anyone have any questions?

  OK. I enjoyed meeting you today and look forward to our group. See you all next week.

SESSION REFERENCES

Group Contract Practice Sheet: Kadden et al., 1992; Monti et al., 2002.

56   *Introduction to ADAPT*

HOW DO I SOLVE PROBLEMS?
The 4-Ws Problem-Solving Model

Session Goals

- Students learn that everyone experiences problems.
- Students learn that different types of problems require different solutions.
- Students learn to solve problems using the 4-Ws Problem-Solving Model.

Session Preparation

1. Quickly review the Session Outline.
2. Study the Sample Session and sample dialogue to help you anticipate how your students might respond to content.
3. You may wish to repeat this session with student examples or different scenarios because students will use a problem-solving component in every ADAPT session.

Materials

- Extra copies of ADAPT Contract (Reproducible 1-2)
- Presentation copy of the 4-Ws to Solve Problems (Reproducible 2-1). *Note*: Project on a document camera or enlarge (129% on 11" x 17" paper).
- For each student, one copy of the Session 2 Practice Sheet, 4-Ws to Solve Problems (Reproducible 2-2)
- Whiteboard and dry-erase markers
- Pencils for students to use during session

ABOUT THIS SKILL

Effective problem solving is an important developmental skill for teens. The 4-Ws Problem-Solving Model provides students with a clear, effective problem-solving process.

The problem-solving skills taught in this lesson are part of the foundational skills of the ADAPT program.

SESSION OUTLINE

BEGINNING THE SESSION

1 **Welcome students, ask for questions, and review contract goals.**

- Review contract goals.
  Provide additional contracts (Reproducible 1-2) as needed and have students complete them during the session.
- If anyone had difficulty generating two goals, ask the group to help.

2 **Have students sign their contracts and turn them in to you.** Explain that you will countersign, make copies, and return them at the next session.

PRESENTING THE TOPIC & PRACTICING SKILLS

Problem-Solving Skills

1 **Introduce the topic of problem solving.** Explain to students that experiencing problems is a normal part of life.

2 **Discuss the difference between small problems and large problems—large problems are more difficult to solve.**

3 **Emphasize that effective problem solving is a skill that can be learned.**

If a student claims to already be a good problem solver, acknowledge the student by saying, "I appreciate that. Your contributions and ideas will help us all." It is important to be genuine and avoid any hint of sarcasm. The goal is to engage all students—even the resistant ones.

4 **Discuss three mistakes that can make it difficult to solve a problem.**
- Failing to examine the problem
- Failing to identify solutions
- Trying to solve a problem with a poor or impulsive choice

5 **Have students identify people who are good and bad problem solvers and then describe characteristics of each.**
- Good problem solvers:
    1. Recognize problems while they are still small.
    2. Solve small problems before they become large problems.
    3. Follow through on a good solution to a problem.
- Bad problem solvers:
    1. Avoid problems or fail to recognize them.
    2. Select a solution impulsively.
    3. Select solutions that are not the best.
- Summarize the characteristics of good problem solvers.

6 **Display and discuss the 4-Ws to Solve Problems (Reproducible 2-1).** Explain that you will go through and practice each problem-solving step.

Step 1: **W**hat is the problem?
Step 2: **W**hat are your options to solve it?

> Students often think they have very limited choices when dealing with challenging problems, which can lead to feelings of hopelessness. This step helps students understand that they always have more options than they initially considered.

Step 3: **W**hat solution do I choose?
Step 4: **W**hat worked?

STEP 1: What is the problem?
- First, identify that a problem exists by recognizing physical cues and observing others.
- Second, understand the problem clearly.

Write these four tips to understand a problem on the board for easy reference:
1. Who is involved in the problem?
2. How did the problem start?
3. How long has the problem been going on?
4. How can the problem be broken into manageable steps?

- Third, don't avoid the problem.
- Use student-generated examples to practice Step 1.

Wait for student responses. You can prompt students by asking, "What is the last problem you dealt with?" If students still have difficulty responding, call on a student or suggest some common problems such as suspension from school, not completing homework or a major assignment, being late for curfew, or being offered a drug by a friend.

Presenting the Lessons

Reproducibles that you can use as visual aids for many ADAPT activities are provided on the CD. Alternatively, you can present and work through activities using a whiteboard.

ADAPT: Advancing Decision Making and Problem Solving for Teens

SESSION OUTLINE

STEP 2: What are your options to solve it?

- Discuss several methods to generate potential solutions, such as:
  - Brainstorming
  - Giving yourself advice
  - Thinking about advice from others
  - Thinking about past problems
- Practice this step using student-generated examples.

 ADAPT Tip As students generate possible options for solving a problem, write their responses on the board for use in Step 3.

STEP 3: What solution do you choose?

- Identify positive and negative outcomes for each potential solution.
- Number the solutions from first (most realistic) to last (least realistic).

STEP 4: What worked?

- Try your best solution.
- Ask, "Did it work?" Remember, some solutions take time to work.
- If the solution didn't work, go back to your list of potential solutions and try your second-best solution, or go back to Step 2 of the 4-Ws and generate more potential solutions.

Practice Sheet Icon

Tell students that the picture of the pencil indicates a writing assignment.

ENDING THE SESSION

1 Have students discuss what they found most helpful about using the 4-Ws for problem solving and what might be difficult.

2 Pass out the Session 2 Practice Sheet, the 4-Ws to Solve Problems (Reproducible 2-2).

- Guide students through the activity and answer any questions.
- Tell students that their practice sheets are due at the beginning of the next session.

How Do I Solve Problems?

SAMPLE SESSION

SESSION 2

BEGINNING THE SESSION

1 **Welcome students, ask for questions, and review contract goals.**

Welcome back to the group! Does anyone have reactions or questions about the program or the material from our last session? Jamal? Yeah, I'm still not clear what I will get out of this program.

I'm glad you brought that up. I want to make sure everyone feels like they are getting something out of our time. Let's review the goals on your ADAPT Contracts to see whether the ADAPT sessions target things that will help you meet your goals. Jamal, does that sound OK? Sure.

ADAPT Guideline

Sample scripts are intended to help you visualize the lesson in advance. Remember to use your own words to convey the information.

- Review contract goals.
  Provide additional contracts (Reproducible 1-2) as needed and have students complete them during the session.

  Everyone, get out your contracts. Let's look at your goals. Ryan, what are your goals? Not smoking so much and talking about things when I have a problem instead of isolating myself.

  Great, Ryan. We are going to cover several topics that will help you with those goals. You've already started on your second goal—just sharing in group is a start.

  Jamal, would you mind sharing your goals so I can figure out whether we can make these sessions worth your time . . .

- If anyone had difficulty generating two goals, ask the group to help.

  Maria, what goals do you have?
  I couldn't think of any.

  Not a problem. Let's go around the group. Then we can brainstorm some ideas with you. Some of the others may have goals that would work for you, too.

2 **Have students sign their contracts and turn them in to you.**
Explain that you will countersign, make copies, and return them at the next session.

ADAPT: Advancing Decision Making and Problem Solving for Teens

SESSION 2

SAMPLE SESSION

PRESENTING THE TOPIC & PRACTICING SKILLS

Problem-Solving Skills

1 **Introduce the topic of problem solving.** Explain to students that experiencing problems is a normal part of life.

Today we are going to talk about how to solve problems effectively. These are important skills to learn because it is a normal part of life to experience problems. Problems become more challenging when we don't have effective strategies for solving them.

2 **Discuss the difference between small problems and large problems—large problems are more difficult to solve.**

Some problems are small and easily solved. Others are big and harder to solve. An example of a small problem would be deciding if you would rather play basketball or skateboard after school. An example of a larger problem is explaining to your teacher why you didn't do your homework.

What are some other examples of small problems? Angie? Like, what to wear . . . Exactly.

Small problems are easy to solve. We usually don't think too much about them or get stressed out about them. Larger problems, however, are more difficult to solve and usually more stressful. What are some examples of larger or more difficult problems? Will? Being offered drugs at a party.

I would say that is a large problem. Who has another example? A friend asking you to skip school with him . . .
Jamal—good example of a large problem. Thanks for sharing.

Think about this scenario. Imagine you are on probation and are randomly given drug tests. Your probation officer has told you that he will send you to detention the next time your drug test is dirty. What do you think? Big or small problem? What might you do in that situation?

Megan? Well, it's a big problem and probably stupid to have gotten into it. I don't know. It sounds like the kid is heading toward detention.

You are right, Megan.
This is a large problem, and large problems are more difficult to solve.
That's what we are going to tackle in this session and the next.

62   *How Do I Solve Problems?*

3 **Emphasize that effective problem solving is a skill that can be learned.**

If a student claims to already be a good problem solver, acknowledge the student by saying, "I appreciate that. Your contributions and ideas will help us all." It is important to be genuine and avoid any hint of sarcasm. The goal is to engage all students—even the resistant ones.

Some people are better at solving their problems than others. Some of us may feel like we have more than our share of problems. That may be true, but the good news is this: Effective problem solving is a skill that can be learned.

4 **Discuss three mistakes that can make it difficult to solve a problem.**

- Failing to examine the problem
- Failing to identify solutions
- Trying to solve a problem with a poor or impulsive choice

5 **Have students identify people who are good and bad problem solvers and then describe characteristics of each.**

- Good problem solvers:
    1. Recognize problems while they are still small.
    2. Solve small problems before they become large problems.
    3. Follow through on a good solution to a problem.

You all probably know people who are good at problem solving.
Who are people you know who are good at solving problems? Maria?
My dad is good at solving problems.

What makes him good at it? He decides on a good solution and then does it. He doesn't worry about it so much like I do.

So, he follows through on a good solution to a problem and doesn't waver or second-guess himself. Yeah, that sounds right.

As you get more practice and experience effectively solving problems, it will be easier to determine the best solution—like your dad, Maria.

You'll also have more confidence in following through on the solution you choose. Not being confident usually tells you that you are not 100% sure that you chose the best solution to the problem.

Think about this. What makes people good at solving problems in general? Ryan? When they don't let their problems get out of control . . .

What do you mean? I mean dealing with something before it becomes a larger problem.

ADAPT: Advancing Decision Making and Problem Solving for Teens   **63**

SAMPLE SESSION

It sounds like you're saying that solving smaller problems is easier and can prevent bigger problems. Yeah, they don't ignore the small stuff—they deal with it.

Yes, that sounds like an important part of effective problem solving.

- Bad problem solvers:
    1. Avoid problems or fail to recognize them.
    2. Select a solution impulsively.
    3. Select solutions that are not the best.

You also probably know people who are bad at solving problems. Who are people you know who are bad at solving problems? Megan? My uncle is really bad at solving problems.

What makes you say that? Well, he is always making his life harder because he chooses the wrong way to handle things.

So, the solutions he chooses are not always the best ones? Yeah, that's one way to say it. He makes more problems for himself. Like he gets lonely, so then he starts drinking.

By not choosing the best solutions he creates more problems for himself? Exactly.

Yes, an important part of effective problem solving is choosing good solutions that are more likely to work.

What makes people bad at solving problems in general? Will? When they don't choose good solutions, like Megan said.

What else? When they don't think about what they do before they do it.

Do you mean when someone solves a problem with the first thing that comes to mind or decides on a solution impulsively without really thinking through the problem? Yep.

- Summarize the characteristics of good problem solvers.

    You all came up with good examples of characteristics of effective and not-so-effective problem solvers. Some of the important qualities for effective problem solving include recognizing that solving smaller problems helps prevent larger problems, thinking through good solutions before choosing one, and being confident in the solution you choose.

    Becoming an effective problem solver takes time and work, but the outcomes are always better than ignoring the problem or choosing bad solutions to problems. You are always going to have problems in your life, just like everyone else. So why not solve problems in ways that will benefit you? Now we are going to spend some time practicing specific skills that you can use to effectively solve problems.

64 *How Do I Solve Problems?*

SESSION 2

 Display and discuss the 4-Ws to Solve Problems (Reproducible 2-1).
Explain that you will go through and practice each problem-solving step.

Step 1: **W**hat is the problem?

Step 2: **W**hat are your options to solve it?

> Students often think they have very limited choices when dealing with challenging problems, which can lead to feelings of hopelessness. This step helps students understand that they always have more options than they initially considered.

Step 3: **W**hat solution do you choose?

Step 4: **W**hat worked?

Presenting the Lessons

Reproducibles that you can use as visual aids for many ADAPT activities are provided on the CD. Alternatively, you can present and work through activities using a whiteboard.

STEP 1: What is the problem?

- First, identify that a problem exists by recognizing physical cues and observing others.

    At first, people don't always recognize that a problem exists, but there are usually clues. Your body may feel different—tense, stressed, or angry. Your behavior may also change. For example, you may avoid others and want to be by yourself. Your thoughts may also change. You may think things like, "I can't do anything right." Finally, when a problem exists, other people may also notice differences in you and say things like, "You are acting differently. Is something wrong?"

    Does any of this relate to your experiences? Angie? My stomach always gets upset when I have a big problem to deal with.

    Do you always connect an upset stomach to having a problem?
    No, not always, but my stomach usually always feels better when I deal with the problem.

    Who else has experienced any of these things? Megan? I guess I get down on myself and tell myself that I can't do anything right.

    How does that make your body feel when you tell yourself things like that? My body usually feels bad. I feel sad and angry at myself at the same time.

    Those are both good examples of recognizing that a problem exists.

- Second, understand the problem clearly.

 Write these four tips to understand a problem on the board for easy reference:
  1. Who is involved in the problem?
  2. How did the problem start?
  3. How long has the problem been going on?
  4. How can the problem be broken into manageable steps?

ADAPT: Advancing Decision Making and Problem Solving for Teens   65

SESSION 2

SAMPLE SESSION

After you recognize that a problem exists, it's important to understand as much about the problem as possible. For example, ask yourself, "Who is involved in the problem? How did it start? How long has it been going on?" If you examine the problem closely, it will often seem more manageable and less stressful. It's often easier to manage small parts of a problem than to find a solution to everything at once.

- Third, don't avoid the problem.

  Some people recognize problems but try to ignore them or downplay their importance. Acting overconfident doesn't resolve a problem, nor does distracting yourself. What are some ways teens might try to distract themselves from a problem? They party. Sometimes they drink or smoke. I know some guys who . . .

- Use student-generated examples to practice this step.

  Ok, now we are going to practice Step 1 of the 4-Ws: What is the problem? to see how it works with real problems. What are some of the common problems that you deal with?

Wait for student responses. You can prompt students by asking, "What is the last problem you dealt with?" If students still have difficulty responding, call on a student or suggest some common problems such as suspension from school, not completing homework or a major assignment, being late for curfew, or being offered a drug by a friend.

Let's spend a few minutes learning how to recognize and understand a problem. Maria, you shared with us that you recently had a big problem at home with your Mom. How did you know that there was a problem? Because I didn't want to go home.

Our first question is, "Who is involved in the problem?" So, your mom was involved. Was anyone else? Her boyfriend.

How did the problem start? It started when they started seeing each other and he started coming over.

How long has it been going on? Since November—about three months.

OK, let's break the problem down. Is the problem your mother's boyfriend? No, I mean not really. He is an OK guy and I want my mom to be happy.

Then what is it? Well, it started OK because he only came over a couple times a week, but then he started coming over almost every day. It used to be just me and my mom. I liked it that way.

The problem sounds like it is related to how much her boyfriend is at your house. Yeah, that's about it.

66 How Do I Solve Problems?

So, if the boyfriend would leave, everything would be OK?
Yes. I mean no. That really wouldn't solve it because I want my mom to be happy and I really don't dislike him.

Then what? I guess it would be better if he would come over less.

How would that help? I would want to be at home more because I like it there.

So, by examining the problem more closely, it seems like the real problem is how much time your mom's boyfriend spends at your house? Yeah, I guess so.

OK, that seems more manageable to deal with because you have identified the specific problem. Now let's talk about some of the things you can do about the problem.

STEP 2: What are your options to solve it?

Students often think they have very limited choices when dealing with challenging problems, which can lead to feelings of hopelessness. Step 2 helps students understand that they always have more options than they initially considered.

- Discuss several methods to generate potential solutions, such as:
  - Brainstorming
  - Giving yourself advice
  - Thinking about advice from others
  - Thinking about past problems

Once you've identified a problem and broken it down, you can determine what choices you have to solve the problem. You may feel hopeless if you don't have options to consider. Our goal is to help you identify your options for solving any problem. Here are some strategies for generating possible solutions to a problem.

*1. **Brainstorming.** Brainstorming is an effective way to figure out your options. First, write down all the possible options or solutions you can think of to solve a problem. Write them down regardless of how good or bad you think they are. You can also ask others—a friend, parent, or teacher—to help you generate solutions. Your goal is to come up with a list of at least four to six possible options. It's even better if you can come up with more. If brainstorming doesn't work, try these strategies.*

*2. **Giving Yourself Advice.** Imagine that your best friend has the same problem. What advice would you give to your friend to help solve it?*

*3. **Thinking of Advice from Others.** Imagine asking your best friend or a trusted adult how to solve the problem. What do you think their advice would be?*

*4. **Thinking About Past Problems.** Have you experienced similar problems in the past? What did you do to solve them?*

ADAPT: Advancing Decision Making and Problem Solving for Teens **67**

SAMPLE SESSION

- Practice this step using student-generated examples.

ADAPT Tip: As students generate possible options to a problem, write their responses on the board for use in Step 3.

Maria, let's go back to talking about the problem you mentioned at home with your mom and her boyfriend. Is that OK? Yeah, sure.

I'm going to ask others in the group to help us generate a list of potential solutions to the problem. As we do this, I will write them on the board.
Maria, why don't you start? Well, I guess I could ask Mom not to see him, but I've already said I don't want her to be lonely and he isn't too bad.

Let's not think about whether it will work yet. Our goal right now is to generate possible solutions. Who else has ideas?

Ask her mom to get another boyfriend.
Move somewhere else.
Talk with her mom about the problem.
Never go home again.
Deal with it and stay in her room.
Go live with her dad.
Talk to her dad and ask him to talk with her mom.

Megan, what would you tell your best friend to do in this situation?
Well, if she wanted her mom to be happy and she really doesn't dislike the boyfriend, I would tell her to talk with her mom about it.

OK, we've generated some potential solutions. Now let's decide how to choose one of them.

STEP 3: What solution do you choose?

- Identify positive and negative outcomes for each potential solution.

Let's look at your potential solutions for dealing with Maria's problem.
We can evaluate each option to determine whether it would be effective. Think about the possible positive and negative outcomes for each.
We can cross out solutions that don't seem realistic at all.
We can also add solutions that are not on the list. Then we can number the remaining solutions from most to least realistic.

First, Maria, is there anything on the list that we should cross out because it won't work or is unrealistic? I would probably cross out the first two because the boyfriend is OK and I'm not moving somewhere else.
Anything else? Never go home again would also not work.
Anything else? No.

How Do I Solve Problems?

Let's evaluate the potential solutions that remain on the list. Do you think talking with your mom about the problem would work? Well, my mom is pretty easy to talk to and she is always telling me to talk with her about what is bothering me.

So, that's a possibility. Yes, I guess it is.

What about dealing with it and staying in your room? I tried that for a while and I get tired of staying in my room, but it does help when I need a break from her boyfriend.

So, it's something you have tried before and could do again, but probably not a long-term solution? Yeah.

What about going to live with your dad? Living with Dad is OK, but I like living with my mom better.

It's something you could try if you needed to, but it's not your number-one choice? Yeah.

What about talking with your dad and asking him to talk with your mom? I talk to Dad about problems, but I don't think asking Dad to talk with my mom would be good because they don't get along that well.

So talking with your dad about problems is an option, but asking him to talk with your mom is probably not the best idea? Yeah, you said it.

- Number the solutions from first (most realistic) to last (least realistic).
  Now, let's number the options that remain on the list from most to least realistic, using 1 for the most realistic option.
  I think talking with my mom would be a good place to start for the reasons I've already mentioned. That will be number 1.

  Then, I could probably talk with my dad and see if he has any ideas, but I wouldn't ask him to talk with Mom. That will be number 2, and I will cross out "and ask him to talk with Mom."

  I guess stay in my room is always an option at times when I just need a break. OK, that will be number 3. Sounds like that option may work in the short term but is probably not a long-term option?
  Yeah, I guess not.

  I could always go live with my dad if things got too unbearable at home. That will be number 4. Sounds like that option is probably a last resort, but still a possibility? Yeah, I guess so.

  So, it sounds like talking with your mom is probably the best place to start for trying to solve this problem? Is that something you see yourself being able to do?
  Yeah, I could do that.

ADAPT: Advancing Decision Making and Problem Solving for Teens

SAMPLE SESSION

STEP 4: What worked?

- Try your best solution.

  For Step 4, you try your best solution. Maria, are you willing to try the first thing on your list and then report back to us how it went at our next group session? Yeah, I guess I can do that.

  I really appreciate your willingness to do this. Let me know if you need any help figuring out how to start the conversation. OK, I think I can do it.

- Ask, "Did it work?" Remember, some solutions take time to work.

  After you've tried a solution, evaluate how well it worked. Ask yourself, "Did it solve the problem?" If your solution worked, that's great! You will know how to solve similar problems in the future. If the problem wasn't completely resolved, ask yourself, "Did it improve the situation?" Remember, some solutions may take time to work. They won't be solved immediately. A problem may be resolved just a little bit at a time.

- If the solution didn't work, go back to your list of potential solutions and try your second-best or realistic solution, or go back to Step 2 of the 4-Ws and generate more potential solutions.

  Also remember that you still have other options to try on the list if the first one really doesn't work. We can talk more about how it went next time and go from there. Does that sound OK to you? Yeah.

  For those of you who shared a problem today, you can use that problem on the practice sheet that is due at the beginning of the next group session.

ENDING THE SESSION

 Have students discuss what they found most helpful about using the 4-Ws for problem solving and what might be difficult.

Before we end today, I want to know what you thought about the 4-Ws problem-solving approach we discussed. Specifically, what do you like about it and what may be hard to do?

SESSION 2

2 **Pass out the Session 2 Practice Sheet, the 4-Ws to Solve Problems (Reproducible 2-2).**

- Guide students through the activity and answer questions.

    Your 4-Ws to Solve Problems Practice Sheet has four questions that you need to complete. The first question asks you to identify a problem that occurs this week. You can also use a problem that already happened. If you shared a problem today, you can use that.

    The second question asks you to write down your options for solving the problem. The third question asks you to identify your best choice for solving the problem. The last question asks you to describe how your solution worked.

    There is a picture of a pencil next to the space where you answer will go. The pencil means that you need to write in that section to complete it. Are there any questions?

- Tell students that their practice sheets are due at the beginning of the next session.

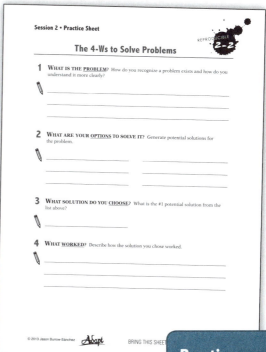

Practice Sheet Icon

Tell students that the picture of the pencil indicates a writing assignment.

SESSION REFERENCES

Problem-Solving Method: Bedell, Archer, & Marlow, 1980; D'Zurilla & Goldfried, 1971; Monti et al., 2002; Webb et al., 2002.

Practice Sheet: Monti et al., 2002; Webb et al., 2002.

ADAPT: Advancing Decision Making and Problem Solving for Teens **71**

WHY DO THINGS HAPPEN TO ME?
Decision-Making Chains

SESSION 3

Session Goals

- Students learn to use a decision-making chain to trace how problems develop.
- Students learn to recognize that small and seemingly harmless decisions can lead to negative consequences.
- Students learn that good decisions can prevent problems from happening.

Session Preparation

1. Quickly review the Session Outline.
2. Study the Sample Session and sample dialogue to help you anticipate how your students might respond to content.
3. Review your Session 2 examples and identify students you need to follow up with.
4. Familiarize yourself with Miguel's Scenario (see pp. 79–81) so you can use it to introduce Decision-Making Chains.
5. Students may not want to share personal examples when you practice using Decision-Making Chains, so be prepared to use Alex's School Scenario and Dean's Drug Scenario on p. 83 and p. 84, respectively.

Materials

- For each student, one copy of the Session 3 Practice Sheet, Decision-Making Chains (Reproducible 3-1)
- Whiteboard and dry-erase markers

ABOUT THIS SKILL

Adolescents are prone to think that bad things just happen to them. They fail to recognize that they are active participants in most situations.

This session builds on the 4-Ws to Solve Problems taught in Session 2 and lays the groundwork for Session 4, Why Do I Do That? Part I.

73

SESSION OUTLINE

BEGINNING THE SESSION

1 Welcome students and return countersigned contracts.

2 Review last session's practice sheets.
- Discuss two or three student examples of problem solving.
- Clarify any of the 4-W steps that may not have been clear to students.

3 Follow up with students who worked through the 4-W process in the last session.

Practice Sheet Completion
- Acknowledge successes—completed practice sheets.
- Address challenges—lost or incomplete practice sheets.
- Summarize steps to successful completion.

PRESENTING THE TOPIC & PRACTICING SKILLS

Decision-Making Chains

1 **Remind students that you have discussed how to solve problems *after* the problem already happened.** Then introduce the topic for today—how to *prevent* problems from happening in the first place.

2 **Draw the first row of a blank Decision-Making Chain on the whiteboard (see diagram on p. 78).** Introduce the Decision-Making Chain as a tool to help students answer the question, "Why do I have problems?"

3 **Using Miguel's Scenario, guide students through the Decision-Making Chain.** Work backward from the crossed-out oval. (*Note*: The final Decision-Making Chain will look like Figure 3-1.)

4 **Draw the second row of the chain on the whiteboard, as shown in Figure 3-1.** Illustrate how a different decision could have prevented the problem by writing "Went back to class" in the first box, "Did class work" in the second box, and "Stays in school" in the oval.

74   *Why Do Things Happen To Me?*

Figure 3-1
Completed Decision-Making Chain

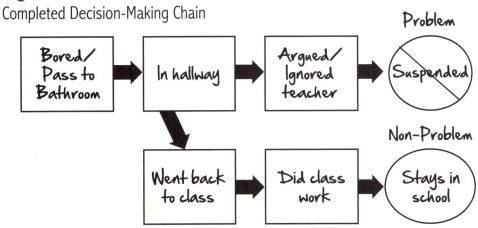

5 **Summarize.**
- Decisions are connected and can lead to unexpected negative consequences.
- Paying attention to thoughts can help you take control.
- Early decision making means stopping to consider the possible consequences of a decision before making it.

6 **Practice session skills.**
- Have students generate examples to illustrate the steps of the Decision-Making Chain.
  Note: Using actual student examples makes the material more real for students. If students aren't comfortable using their own examples, use one of the sample scenarios provided on p. 83 and p. 84 in this session.
- Have students work through the Decision-Making Chain for each problem.
  1. Work backward through the problem.
  2. Have students help you determine what thoughts or behaviors should go in each box or shape.
  3. Have students brainstorm alternative thoughts or behaviors that could have led to more positive outcomes. Draw the alternatives in the second row of the chain.
  4. Have students identify decision(s) made prior to the problem that would have been easiest to change.
  5. Work forward through the chain and have students discuss how to make different choices as the decisions get harder.

ADAPT: Advancing Decision Making and Problem Solving for Teens

SESSION OUTLINE

ENDING THE SESSION

1 **Have students clarify what they learned.**
- Ask students what they found most helpful about the Decision-Making Chains.
- Ask students how they might use the Decision-Making Chain.

2 **Pass out the Session 3 Practice Sheet, Decision-Making Chains (Reproducible 3-1).**
- Explain that practicing the skills between group sessions is important in order to effectively master the skills.
- Remind students that their practice sheets are due at the beginning of the next group session, where they will be reviewed in the group.

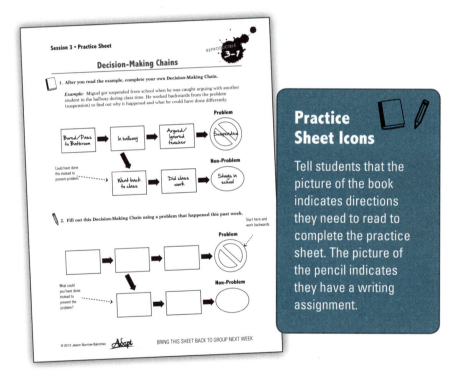

Practice Sheet Icons

Tell students that the picture of the book indicates directions they need to read to complete the practice sheet. The picture of the pencil indicates they have a writing assignment.

76   *Why Do Things Happen To Me?*

SAMPLE SESSION

SESSION 3

BEGINNING THE SESSION

1 Welcome students and return countersigned contracts.

2 Review last session's practice sheets.
- Discuss two or three student examples of problem solving.
- Clarify any of the 4-W steps that may not have been clear to students.

3 Follow up with students who worked through the 4-W process in the last session.

I want to follow up with Maria. Is that OK, Maria? Yes.

To briefly summarize, last week you felt your mother's boyfriend was spending too much time at your house. We talked about potential solutions, and then you numbered them from most to least realistic for solving the problem. You decided that talking with your mom was the best place to start. How did that go? Well, I did talk with her and explained how I felt.

What happened? Mom listened and said that she thought I had been acting differently. She even thanked me for telling her how I felt. She said that she would ask her boyfriend to come over less. She said maybe the three of us could do some things together so that I could get to know him better. I'm not sure why I didn't talk to her before.

How does all that sound to you? Good. I mean, I feel better after talking with her, so I guess it was worth it.

I'm glad you feel better. Your problem solving paid off. Keep monitoring things and see how it goes. Many problems aren't solved at once and require continued work. You have other things on your list of potential solutions, but it sounds like talking with your mom was an effective way to start. Keep us updated on how this goes for you. OK.

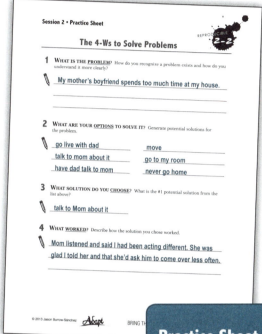

Practice Sheet Completion
- Acknowledge successes—completed practice sheets.
- Address challenges—lost or incomplete practice sheets.
- Summarize steps to successful completion.

ADAPT: Advancing Decision Making and Problem Solving for Teens   77

SAMPLE SESSION

PRESENTING THE TOPIC & PRACTICING SKILLS

Decision-Making Chains

1 **Remind students that you have discussed how to solve problems** *after* **the problem already happened.** Then introduce the topic for today—how to *prevent* problems from happening in the first place.

Today, we'lll talk about how to prevent problems from occurring by understanding how they develop.

Imagine that you have a toolbox. The things you learn in ADAPT are like putting tools in your toolbox. Last week, you learned the 4-Ws to Solve Problems. That tool helps you solve problems after you recognize they exist.

Now we are going to think about preventing problems—stopping them from happening. Sometimes, you can prevent problems if you understand how they develop. We are going to use a Decision-Making Chain to help you learn to prevent problems.

Here's a way to think about the ADAPT tools. Last week we used the 4-W tool to answer the question, "How do I solve problems?" This week we will answer the question, "Why do problems or things happen to me?" The tool we will use is called a Decision-Making Chain.

2 **Draw the first row of a blank Decision-Making Chain on the whiteboard.** Introduce the Decision-Making Chain as a tool to help students answer the question, "Why do I have problems?"

This is called a Decision-Making Chain.

The chain will help us trace how things happen and answer the question "Why do problems happen to me?" Sometimes teens find themselves in situations that they didn't see coming—situations that have negative consequences like getting referred to the office or suspended.

It's easy to think you are a victim. It's easy to think things like "I didn't mean to get suspended—it just happened" or "I didn't mean to smoke weed at the party—it just happened." Have you ever heard anyone say things like this?

78   *Why Do Things Happen To Me?*

SESSION 3

3 **Using Miguel's Scenario, guide students through the Decision-Making Chain.** Work backward from the crossed-out oval. (*Note*: The final Decision-Making Chain will look like the figure below.)

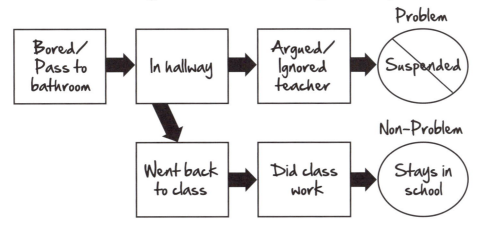

I'm going to tell you a story about Miguel, and we are going to use the Decision-Making Chain to answer the question, "Why is Miguel experiencing a problem?" To do this, we need to work backwards from the problem itself. Miguel's problem is this—he got suspended.

Write the word "Suspended" in the Problem oval.

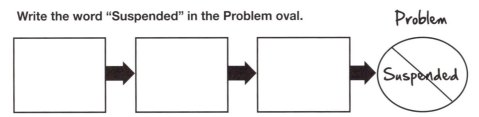

When Miguel's mom found out about the suspension, she asked, "Why did you get suspended"? Miguel said, "It just happened!"

Write "It just happened!" above the chain.

What do you think? Did it just happen? Will? Miguel probably did something stupid.

Let's see. When Miguel completed his suspension, he sat down with his school counselor. The counselor drew a Decision-Making Chain. We already know the negative outcome. What was it? He got suspended.

ADAPT: Advancing Decision Making and Problem Solving for Teens   **79**

SESSION 3

SAMPLE SESSION

Yes, Miguel was suspended. He also told his counselor that it just happened.

Next, the school counselor asked Miguel what happened before he got suspended. Miguel said he was arguing with another student and then a teacher came by. She asked them to go back to class. Miguel said he ignored the teacher and didn't do what she asked him.

Write "Argued/Ignored teacher" in the third box.

The school counselor then asked what happened right before he got into the argument with the other student. Miguel said that he was walking in the hallway.

Write "In hallway" in the second box.

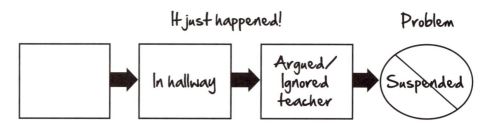

The school counselor then asked what happened right before he was walking in the hallway. Miguel said he got bored in class and asked for a bathroom pass, even though he didn't need to use the bathroom.

Write "Bored/Pass to bathroom" in the first box.

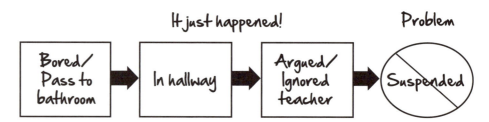

The school counselor looked at Miguel's Decision-Making Chain and said, "So this whole thing started because you were bored in class?"

Miguel said, "Yeah, I guess so."

This is interesting. Let's think about some of the decisions or choices Miguel could have made. What could he have done before the suspension occurred to prevent it?

Why Do Things Happen To Me?

SESSION 3

Jamal? *He should've left the other kid alone. If you are going to be in the hall, best to keep a low profile.*

Good. Ryan? *Bad idea to ignore a teacher. He should've listened.*

So he could have avoided being noticed by not arguing and he could have gone back to class instead of ignoring the teacher. It does sound like that would have prevented the suspension. Let's see how that would look on the Decision-Making Chain.

4 **Draw the second row of a blank chain on the whiteboard, as shown below.** Illustrate how a different decision could have prevented the problem by writing "Went back to class" in the first box, "Did class work" in the second box, and "Stays in school" in the oval.

I'd like you to think about one more thing. Miguel said he was bored in class. How many of you have ever thought, "I'm bored in class?" How many of you have ever thought, "It would be great to leave after third period?"

Your thoughts can lead to actions. It's normal. If I'm tired or having a bad day, I sometimes think the same things. The important thing is to not listen to those thoughts and avoid a chain of negative events.

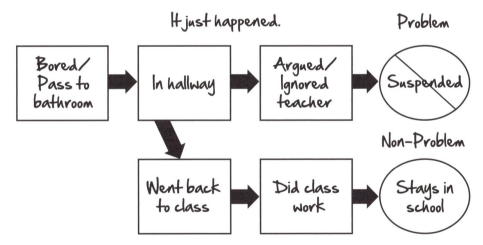

5 **Summarize.**

- Decisions are connected and can lead to unexpected negative consequences.

  Do you think Miguel understood that making the decision to leave class with a bathroom pass would lead to getting suspended? Will? *No. He wasn't thinking that far ahead—he just wanted to get out of class.*

- Paying attention to thoughts can help you take control.

  Paying attention to your thoughts and decisions takes practice.
  Once you know how thoughts and small decisions affect what happens, it will help you take control.

ADAPT: Advancing Decision Making and Problem Solving for Teens

SESSION 3
SAMPLE SESSION

- Early decision making means stopping to consider the possible consequences of a decision before making it. The earlier students make alternative decisions, the easier it will be to avoid problems associated with poor decisions.

  Let's talk just a bit about where Miguel could have made different decisions by first thinking about consequences. He might have followed the teacher's direction if he had thought about what would happen if he ignored her direction. What else? He could've stayed in class.

  Think about this. Which decision resulted in the greatest risk for Miguel to make additional mistakes? Maria? He just should've stayed in class. Kids get in trouble all the time when they hang out in the halls or bathrooms.

  You are very perceptive. Also consider that poor decisions made later in the chain are usually associated with more negative consequences.

 Practice session skills.

- Have students generate examples to illustrate the steps in the Decision-Making Chain.
  Note: Using actual student examples makes the material more real for students. If students aren't comfortable using their own examples, use either Alex's School Scenario or Dean's Drug Scenario provided on the following pages.
- Have students work through the Decision-Making Chain for each problem.
  1. Work backward through the problem. As in real life, there are multiple negative outcomes in the scenarios. For simplicity, focus at first on the major negative outcome.
  2. Have students help you determine what thoughts or behaviors should go in each box.
  3. Have students brainstorm alternative thoughts or behaviors that could have led to more positive outcomes. Draw the alternatives in the second row of boxes.
  4. Have students identify decision(s) made prior to the problem that would have been easiest to change.
  5. Work forward through the chain and have students discuss how to make different choices as the decisions get harder.

82   *Why Do Things Happen To Me?*

SESSION
3

ALEX'S SCHOOL SCENARIO

Student Example

About a month ago, Alex, his parents, the principal, and the school counselor met to discuss Alex's attendance and ways to improve it. Following that discussion, Alex has had good school attendance and everyone is feeling positive.

Unfortunately, Alex still has thoughts that lead to negative results. Today, when he arrives at school, Alex sees his friend Sam in the hallway. Sam often says things like, "School is a waste of time." Many times in the past, Sam has encouraged Alex to leave school early. Alex knows that he has a hard time saying "no" to Sam.

When Alex sees Sam, he thinks to himself, "I wonder what Sam is up to. I haven't talked to him in a while." Then Alex strolls over to meet Sam.

Sam greets Alex with a typical invitation to skip school. "Hey man, let's take off after third period today. We haven't hung out in a while."

At first, Alex resists. "I can't," he says. "Everyone is on my case about missing school."

Sam says, "Too bad, man, we could have a good time."

Alex says to himself, "I haven't skipped class in a long time. If I come back after lunch, it won't be a big deal."

As it turns out, Alex does not return after lunch, but misses the rest of the school day. When Alex arrives home, his mother has already been notified by the counselor that he did not attend all of his classes. Alex's mother is angry with him, and they argue. The next day at school, Alex has to talk with the counselor and explain why he left school. He didn't complete his assignments for classes and his teachers are also upset with him. Alex's parents, the counselor, and his teachers are all angry and disappointed because they had all made an effort to help Alex.

ADAPT: Advancing Decision Making and Problem Solving for Teens   **83**

SESSION 3

SAMPLE SESSION

Student Example

DEAN'S DRUG SCENARIO

Dean has not been smoking marijuana since he got busted two months ago. Dean's probation officer (PO) gives him random urine analysis tests (UAs) to monitor his drug use. Dean's goal is to not smoke marijuana; however, he sometimes has seemingly harmless thoughts that lead to seemingly harmless decisions.

Last week Dean walked home from school—down 3rd Ave. He knew that the friends he used to smoke with hung out there after school. He said to himself, "I wonder what my friends are up to? It won't hurt to walk by." When Dean walked by his friends, they asked him to smoke with them. At first, Dean resisted and said he needed to go home, but he gave in after a few minutes, telling himself, "A few hits can't do any harm. No one will find out."

Dean ended up hanging out with his friends for a couple of hours. When he got home, his mother was angry because he was late. She could smell marijuana smoke on his clothes. He had promised that he would stop smoking. Dean was too high that evening to complete his homework and did not turn it in the next day. Dean's teachers were upset. Two days later, his PO sprung a UA on him. Dean tested positive for marijuana. His PO was upset, and that led to more problems with the courts for violating his probation.

Why Do Things Happen To Me?

ENDING THE SESSION

1 **Have students clarify what they learned.**
- Ask students what they found most helpful about the Decision-Making Chains.
- Ask students how they might use the Decision-Making Chain.

2 **Pass out the Session 3 Practice Sheet, Decision-Making Chains (Reproducible 3-1).**

I've handed everyone a practice sheet—Decision-Making Chains. On the top is Miguel's example. Use this example as a model for completing your own Decision-Making Chain.

- Explain that practicing the skills between group sessions is important to effectively master the skills.

  On the bottom half of the practice sheet is a blank Decision-Making Chain. Using a problem you experience in the coming week or one you've had in the past, complete the Decision-Making Chain and the alternative chain for preventing the problem. This is a great opportunity for you to practice how decision making works in your own life.
  Are there any questions?

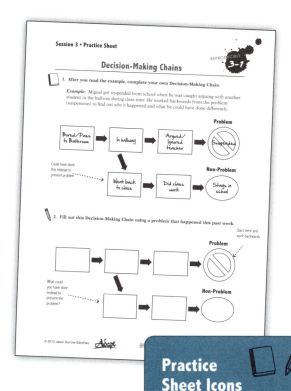

- Remind students that their practice sheets are due at the beginning of the next group session, where they will be reviewed in the group.

Practice Sheet Icons

Tell students that the picture of the book indicates directions they need to read to complete the practice sheet. The picture of the pencil indicates they have a writing assignment.

SESSION REFERENCES
Marlatt and Witkiewitz, 2005; Monti et al., 2002.

WHY DO I DO THAT? PART 1
Mapping and Understanding Problem Behaviors

SESSION 4

Session Goals

- Students learn how triggers, behaviors, and positive and negative consequences are related.
- Students learn to weigh the positive and negative consequences of behaviors.

Session Preparation

1. Quickly review the Session Outline.
2. Study the Sample Session and sample dialogue to help you anticipate how your students might respond to content.
3. Review Jordan's Scenario (pp. 93–96). Use it to explain how to use mapping to understand problem behaviors. If the scenario is not appropriate for your group, choose an example that most students will relate to, such as getting into fights, skipping school, or leaving when arguing with parents.
4. Draw a blank map (see p. 89) on the whiteboard or display Reproducible 4-1.

Materials

- For each student, one copy of:
    - Mapping Problem Behavior (Reproducible 4-1)
    - Session 4 Practice Sheet, Mapping Problem Behavior (Reproducible 4-2)
- Whiteboard and dry-erase markers or a document camera
- Pencils for students to use during session

ABOUT THIS SKILL

Adolescents do not always understand why they engage in certain behaviors, especially problem behaviors that lead to bad consequences. Understanding why they engage in problem behaviors can lead to better outcomes.

Maps provide a simple, functional assessment and give the adolescent a tool for visually tracing antecedents, behaviors, and consequences. Students learn to identify what leads to a behavior and analyze what follows the behavior.

Session 5 builds on this session, focusing on how to use maps to identify positive alternative behaviors.

87

SESSION OUTLINE

BEGINNING THE SESSION

Practice Sheet Completion

- Acknowledge successes—completed practice sheets.
- Address challenges—lost or incomplete practice sheets.
- Summarize steps to successful completion.

Welcome students and review last session's practice sheets. Discuss two or three student practice sheets. Provide clarification as needed.

PRESENTING THE TOPIC & PRACTICING SKILLS

Presenting the Lessons

Reproducibles that you can use as visual aids for many ADAPT activities are provided on the CD. Alternatively, you can present and work through activities using a whiteboard.

Mapping and Understanding Problem Behaviors

1 **Remind students that you have discussed ways to prevent problems by understanding how they develop.** Then introduce the focus for this week—understanding why people do certain behaviors.

2 **Pass out Mapping Problem Behaviors (Reproducible 4-1) and introduce the basic steps in mapping problem behavior.** Display Reproducible 4-1 or draw a blank map on the whiteboard. A completed map, with Jordan's scenario filled in, is shown in Figure 4-1.

See CD for **Reproducible 4-1**

88   *Why Do I Do That? Part 1*

Figure 4-1
Jordan's Scenario

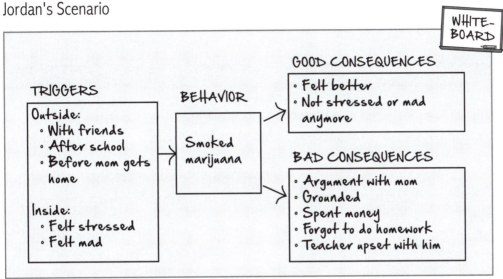

3 **Complete the map using Jordan's Scenario (as shown above) or a student-generated example.**

- Identify the question, "Why did Jordan smoke marijuana?" Then have students fill in the box labeled "Behavior" on their worksheets.
- Discuss Jordan's inside and outside triggers and have students fill in the box labeled "Triggers."
- Discuss the good and bad consequences that resulted from Jordan's marijuana use, and have students fill in the boxes on their maps. Use the sample scenario to help students understand that behaviors often result in *both* good and bad consequences. With problem behaviors, the bad consequences outweigh the good and are also often more enduring than good consequences. Explain that it is important to consider the bad consequences.

4 **Summarize.**

- Review the scenario and explain that you answered the question, "Why did Jordan smoke marijuana?"
- Review how triggers, behaviors, and consequences are connected and why they are important to recognize.
- Encourage students to think about how they can map and understand different problem behaviors in their own lives.
- Acknowledge that understanding problem behaviors is only half of the story and that you will cover alternative positive behaviors in the next session.

ADAPT: Advancing Decision Making and Problem Solving for Teens   **89**

SESSION OUTLINE

5 Depending on the time remaining, map other problem behaviors using student-generated examples.

ENDING THE SESSION

1 **Have students clarify what they have learned.**
- Ask students what they found most helpful about mapping problem behaviors and which parts of the map were difficult to fill out.
- Ask students how they might use mapping to understand problem behaviors.

2 **Pass out the Session 4 Practice Sheet, Mapping Problem Behavior (Reproducible 4-2).**
- Remind students that practicing the skills between group sessions is important in order to master the skills.
- Emphasize that examples can include past drug use, but they don't have to. Make it clear to students that they should not engage in drug use in order to complete the practice sheet.
- Remind students that their practice sheets are due at the next session, when they will be reviewed in the group.

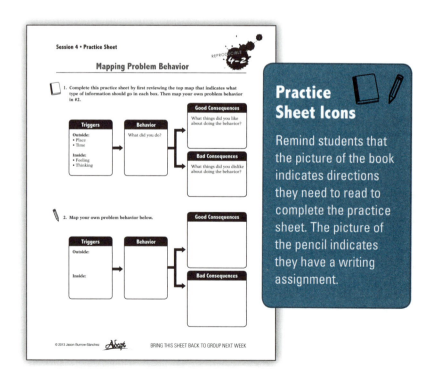

Practice Sheet Icons

Remind students that the picture of the book indicates directions they need to read to complete the practice sheet. The picture of the pencil indicates they have a writing assignment.

Why Do I Do That? Part 1

SAMPLE SESSION

SESSION 4

BEGINNING THE SESSION

Welcome students and review last session's practice sheets. Discuss two or three student practice sheets. Provide clarification as needed.

Welcome back! We are going to start by reviewing the Decision-Making Chains you filled out on your practice sheets.

I look forward to hearing how you analyzed your own problem. I'm especially interested in the alternative behaviors you've identified—behaviors that helped or would have helped you avoid negative consequences. Who would like to start? Megan, thanks. Is it OK to put your chain on the document camera?
Yeah, that's OK.

This looks like a great chain. Why don't you walk us through it?
Well, the first thing that happened was a pop quiz in my lit class. Then I didn't understand a couple of questions. So one of the things I might've done was cheat, and that would have led to detention.

That would be a negative outcome.
Oh yeah, and I would've gotten an F.

I see you also filled in what you could have done instead to prevent going to detention and getting an F. Yes, I could have asked the teacher for help instead of cheating. Actually, that's what I did. Then I finished the test on my own.

Great! So what was the result? No detention.

And your grade? I don't know yet, but I know it was better than an F.

Megan, thank you for sharing your Decision-Making Chain. I like seeing how you are using the thinking process to avoid a potential problem. Who else would like to share?

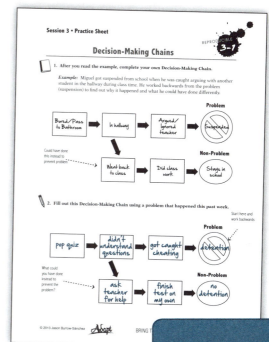

Practice Sheet Completion

- Acknowledge successes—completed practice sheets.
- Address challenges—lost or incomplete practice sheets.
- Summarize steps to successful completion.

PRESENTING THE TOPIC & PRACTICING SKILLS

Mapping and Understanding Problem Behaviors

1 **Remind students that you have discussed ways to prevent problems by understanding how they develop.** Then introduce the focus for this week—understanding why people do certain behaviors.

So far, we've practiced problem solving and decision making. Today we are going to add to what you've learned to find out why people engage in certain behaviors. You can deal with your problems more effectively if you understand <u>why</u> they occur in the first place.

ADAPT: Advancing Decision Making and Problem Solving for Teens **91**

SESSION 4

SAMPLE SESSION

2 **Pass out Mapping Problem Behaviors (Reproducible 4-1) and introduce the basic steps in mapping problem behavior.** Display Reproducible 4-1 or draw a blank map on the whiteboard. A completed map, with Jordan's scenario filled in, is shown in Figure 4-1.

Presenting the Lessons

Reproducibles that you can use as visual aids for many ADAPT activities are provided on the CD. Alternatively, you can present and work through activities using a whiteboard.

Figure 4-1
Jordan's Scenario

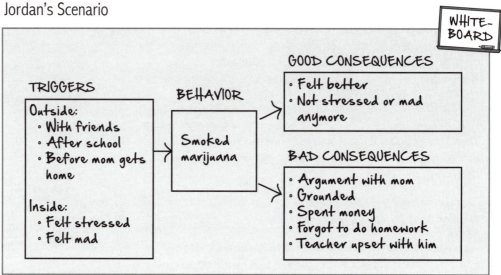

To get at the "why" question, we're going to use a new tool called mapping. It will help us answer the question, "Why do I do certain behaviors?"

Look at the second box labeled "Behavior." The kinds of behaviors we want to understand now are behaviors that cause you problems—for example, skipping school, using drugs, or borrowing your mom's car without asking. What are some other behaviors that you or your friends might have problems with? **Staying out all night, texting in class, getting in fights, shoplifting . . .**

Those are great examples. Mapping will help us look at those kinds of behaviors in ways you may not have thought of. Look at the first box. We're going to look at things that often precede or come before a problem behavior. Those things are called triggers. A trigger is something that starts our behaviors in motion.

There are two types of triggers—inside and outside. Let's think about an outside trigger for smoking marijuana. It could be a place, like a friend's house or a party. An outside trigger could also be the time of day, like after school or Saturday night.

Inside triggers can be a feeling or thought. Being bored can sometimes be an inside trigger. So can being mad, anxious, or sad. An inside trigger for drinking could be a thought like "I'm so angry right now" or "Drinking would make me feel better."

92   Why Do I Do That? Part 1

SESSION 4

Does anyone have questions about what a trigger is—either outside or inside?

Can anyone provide another example of a trigger to a problem behavior? Ryan? Could a trigger be something like being at the park? What do you mean? Well, when I smoked in the past, it was usually at the park after school.

Actually, both of those things, being at the park and after school, qualify as triggers because they are things that come before the behavior and set it in motion. Ryan, you are probably more likely to smoke marijuana when you are at the park. That's a specific place. After school is a specific time of day. So those are both outside triggers.

Any other examples? What about you, Jamal? I guess I've used marijuana when I've been mad.

Yes, being mad would qualify as an inside trigger. We can guess that you are more likely to smoke when you feel mad.

Now look at the last two boxes. Those boxes are for what comes after the behavior. Most problem behaviors have negative and positive consequences. Mapping will help us look at both types of consequences.

3 **Complete the map using Jordan's Scenario (as shown in Figure 4-1) or a student-generated example.**

Student Example

EXAMPLES

Jordan's Scenario is a drug-use example. Such examples will be relevant to many of the students in the program and provide an opportunity to discuss the question, "Why do people use drugs?" However, if the drug-use example is not relevant or appropriate for your group, choose a problem behavior that most students in the group can relate to. Examples include getting into fights, skipping school or class, or leaving when arguing with parents.

- Identify the question, "Why did Jordan smoke marijuana?" Then have students fill in the box labeled "Behavior" on their worksheets.

    To show you how mapping works, we're going to talk about a 15-year-old student named Jordan. We are going to try to answer the question, "Why did Jordan smoke marijuana?" What is the behavior we are going to look at? Angie? Smoking marijuana.

    Look at your map and write "smoking marijuana" in the second box, labeled "Behavior."

ADAPT: Advancing Decision Making and Problem Solving for Teens   **93**

SAMPLE SESSION

- Discuss Jordan's inside and outside triggers and have students fill in the box labeled "Triggers."

Now, let's try to understand Jordan's triggers. Right before he smoked marijuana, Jordan was with some friends—friends he had smoked with before. It was also after school and before his mother got home from work. Are those outside or inside triggers? Maria, what do you think? Those are outside triggers, kind of like what we talked about with Ryan.

Right, those are outside triggers. Under "Outside" in the "Triggers" box, write "with friends, after school, before mom got home."

Jordan said that he was feeling stressed and mad because his teacher had gotten on his case for not finishing his homework. Is that an outside or inside trigger? Jamal, help me out here. He was stressed, so I guess inside.

Yes, that's an inside trigger. Write "felt stressed" and "felt mad" under "Inside" in the "Triggers" box. Are there any questions about why those are outside or inside triggers?

So, we know that Jordan's outside triggers for smoking marijuana are being with friends, after school, and before his mom got home. And the inside triggers? Megan? Being stressed and mad.

- Discuss the good and bad consequences that resulted from Jordan's marijuana use, and have students fill in the boxes on their maps. Use the sample scenario to help students understand that behaviors often result in *both* good and bad consequences. With problem behaviors, the bad consequences outweigh the good and are also often more enduring than good consequences. Explain that it is important to consider the bad consequences.

OK, you understand triggers. Now let's think about what happened after Jordan smoked marijuana. First, he said that he felt better and wasn't mad anymore. Were those good or bad consequences? Ryan? Good.

Yes, he felt better and wasn't mad anymore. Let's write that under "Good Consequences."

Do you think it's OK to look just at the good consequences? Jamal? No. Some bad things probably happened, too.

That's right—when you look only at the good consequences of a behavior, you ignore the negative consequences. This is especially problematic for people who use drugs because they frequently do not look beyond the good consequences they experience from using the drug—and we all know there can be many negative consequences from using drugs.

In Jordan's situation, he did consider the bad things that occurred as a result of smoking marijuana. Afterwards, his mom smelled the marijuana smoke on his clothes. They got into an argument and he got grounded. He spent money he

94 Why Do I Do That? Part 1

was saving to buy a new skateboard on the marijuana. He also forgot to do his homework that night, and his teachers were upset with him the following day. Can anyone relate to these bad consequences?

Will? *Yeah, I've been grounded before for smoking.*

Maria? *My mom and I have had arguments about smoking marijuana.*

I will write what Jordan experienced in the "Bad Consequences" box. Write "argument with mom, grounded, spent money, forgot to do homework, teacher upset with him" in the "Bad Consequences" box.

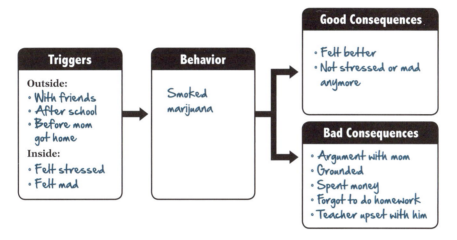

Take a look at the good consequences and bad consequences on the map. What do you notice? Angie? *It's pretty obvious. There are more things in the bad box than in the good box.*

Yes, Jordan experienced more bad consequences from smoking marijuana than good consequences. Here's something else to think about. The bad consequences lasted longer—getting grounded, spending money, teachers being upset with him all day at school, and poorer grades. What did Jordan get from the good consequences? *The high from smoking marijuana . . .*

That's right, but it lasted for only a few hours. We started by saying that mapping will help us answer the question, "Why did Jordan smoke marijuana?" Will, do you think you can answer that now? *I think he smoked because he didn't like feeling stressed. And then he got together with friends who like to smoke.*

I agree. Jordan probably smoked marijuana because he wanted to change the way he was feeling. His inside triggers, being stressed and mad, made him want to feel better. Most people use drugs to change the way they feel or think, and Jordan is no different.

Will, you also said he may have been influenced to smoke because he was with his friends. I would agree. Peer pressure to use drugs is very strong. Jordan's friends may have put pressure on him to smoke, and it may be a habit for them to smoke together.

SAMPLE SESSION

Have any of you used drugs to change the way you feel? Or smoked because others were pressuring you? Jamal? Yeah. I usually smoke marijuana when I'm mad.

What about you, Maria? Well, my friends never want to smoke alone. They always ask me to smoke even if I really don't want to.

It sounds like you both can relate to Jordan's reasons for smoking marijuana.

 Summarize.

- Review the scenario and explain that you answered the question, "Why did Jordan smoke marijuana?"

  After looking at our map, it's not a mystery why Jordan smoked marijuana. He smoked marijuana to change the way he was feeling and what he was thinking. There may also have been added peer pressure from his friends. Mapping can help us understand why people engage in specific behaviors.

- Review how triggers, behaviors, and consequences are connected and why they are important to recognize.

  As you can see from the map, Jordan's triggers, his behavior, and the consequences—both good and bad—were all connected. Understanding how things are connected gives us the opportunity to change our behavior for the better. In other words, the more we know about our behavior, the more control we have over it.

- Encourage students to think about how they can map and understand different problem behaviors in their own lives.

  Each of you can probably apply some part of the mapping process to yourself. I mention this because it is important that you understand how your own triggers, behaviors, and consequences are connected. You can use mapping to understand problem behaviors in your own life. Knowing why you do things will help you make the best decisions you can in different situations.

- Acknowledge that understanding problem behaviors is only half of the story. Explain that you will cover alternative positive behaviors in the next session.

  We spent a lot of time today talking about a problem, or negative behavior. We discussed a behavior that led Jordan to experience more negative consequences than positive consequences. This is only half the story—Jordan could have chosen to engage in a behavior that would have led to more positive consequences. In our next session, we will examine alternative positive behaviors that Jordan could have engaged in—behaviors that could have led to more positive consequences than negative consequences.

 Depending on the time remaining, map other problem behaviors using student-generated examples.

Why Do I Do That? Part 1

ENDING THE SESSION

1 **Have students clarify what they have learned.**

- Ask students what they found most helpful about mapping problem behaviors and which parts of the map were difficult to fill out.

  Before we end today, I want to know what you thought about mapping as a tool for understanding problem behaviors. Specifically, what things do you like about it, and what things do you think will be hard to do?

- Ask students how they might use mapping to understand problem behaviors.

  We used a drug example for our map today, but mapping works to figure out many problem behaviors. Can you think of others that you might map?
  For example, a problem behavior might be getting angry. What are some others?
  Missing curfew, talking back . . .

2 **Pass out the Session 4 Practice Sheet, Mapping Problem Behavior (Reproducible 4-2).**

- Remind students that practicing the skills between group sessions is important to master the skills.
- Emphasize that examples can include past drug use, but they don't have to. Make it clear to students that they should not engage in drug use in order to complete the practice sheet.

  I've handed everyone your next practice sheet—Mapping Problem Behaviors. Look at the example at the top of the page. Use that and the worksheet we filled out in group today as models for completing your own map.

  On the bottom half of the sheet is a blank map. Use a problem behavior that you've experienced in the past or that you experience during the next week. If you choose to use an example of drug use for your map, use an example from your past. You should not use drugs in order to complete this practice sheet.

  Are there any questions?

- Remind students that their practice sheets are due at the next session, where they will be reviewed in the group.

SESSION REFERENCES
Kadden et al., 1992; Meyers & Smith, 1995.

Practice Sheet Icons

Remind students that the picture of the book indicates directions they need to read to complete the practice sheet. The picture of the pencil indicates they have a writing assignment.

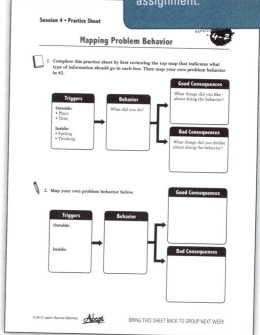

ADAPT: Advancing Decision Making and Problem Solving for Teens

WHY DO I DO THAT? PART II
Mapping Alternative Behaviors

SESSION 5

Session Goals

- Students review the relationships between triggers, behaviors, and positive and negative consequences.
- Students increase their understanding of why problem behaviors occur.
- Students learn how to use positive alternative behaviors in place of problem behaviors to serve the same needs but with better outcomes.

Session Preparation

1. Quickly review the Session Outline.
2. Study the Sample Session and sample dialogue to help you anticipate how your students might respond to content.
3. Draw a completed map on the whiteboard of Jordan's Scenario from the last session. Then draw a blank map below it. If you used a different scenario in Session 4, use that scenario.

Materials

- For each student, one copy of:
  - Mapping Alternative Behaviors (Reproducible 5-1)
  - Session 5 Practice Sheet, Mapping Alternative Behaviors (Reproducible 5-2)
- Whiteboard and dry-erase markers
- Pencils for students to use during session

ABOUT THIS SKILL

When adolescents understand why they engage in problem behaviors, they gain more control over changing them for the better. In order to make lasting behavior changes, they also need to identify positive alternative behaviors that serve the same needs as their problem behaviors.

This session complements the mapping and understanding of problem behaviors taught in Session 4, with the focus on selecting positive alternative behaviors.

99

SESSION OUTLINE

BEGINNING THE SESSION

1 Welcome students.

2 **Review last session's practice sheets.** Discuss two or three student practice sheets.

 Be prepared to spend some time clarifying maps because some students may have found them difficult.

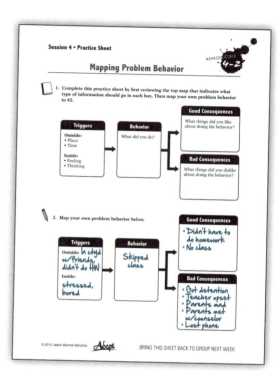

Practice Sheet Completion

- Acknowledge successes—completed practice sheets.
- Address challenges—lost or incomplete practice sheets.
- Summarize steps to successful completion.

PRESENTING THE TOPIC & PRACTICING SKILLS

Mapping Alternative Behaviors

1 **Remind students that the last session focused on understanding *why* people engage in problem behaviors.** This session focuses on selecting positive alternative behaviors that lead to better outcomes.

2 **Pass out the in-session worksheet, Mapping Alternative Behaviors (Reproducible 5-1).** Then quickly review Jordan's Scenario (or the alternative scenario you used) from Session 4 on the whiteboard.

3 **Guide students through another map using skateboarding as the positive alternative behavior.** Fill in each box on the whiteboard. Encourage students to complete their worksheet maps as you discuss the scenario. The completed map will look like Figure 5-1.

Note: The map may seem unrealistic to teens if there are no bad consequences for positive behaviors.

100   Why Do I Do That? Part II

Figure 5-1
Jordan's Alternative Positive Behavior: Skateboarding

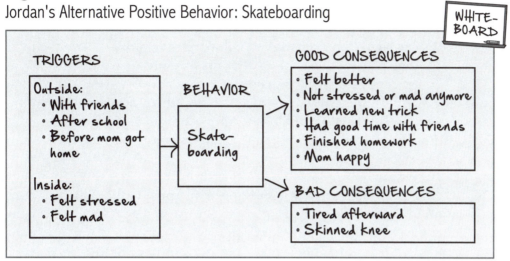

4 **Help students understand two important points about Jordan's alternative behavior:**

1. Jordan experienced more good consequences than bad consequences for skateboarding.
2. Skateboarding led to more good consequences *and* served the same need as the problem behavior—it reduced the feeling of being stressed out and mad. Thus, the question becomes, "Why wouldn't you choose the positive alternative?"

5 **Have students identify eight to ten other positive alternative behaviors for Jordan.** Write their suggestions on the whiteboard.

 If students have difficulty identifying alternative behaviors, have them use the strategies from Session 2—brainstorming, giving yourself advice, thinking about advice from others, and thinking about past problems.

6 **Have students list five positive alternative behaviors they could use for themselves on the backs of their worksheets.** Emphasize that choosing a positive alternative is difficult when you are stressed or angry, so they need to create a list of positive alternative behaviors before they actually need one.

- Have students rank the behaviors on their list from one to five, with one being the most effective.
- Ask students to post their list where they can see it daily.

ADAPT: Advancing Decision Making and Problem Solving for Teens

SESSION OUTLINE

7. Summarize.
- Review Jordan's Scenario. Explain that recognizing triggers (why Jordan smoked marijuana) is an important part of problem solving (finding positive alternative behaviors like skateboarding) that lead to better decisions and outcomes.
- Encourage students to continue thinking about positive alternative behaviors that will work for them.
- Encourage students to use the mapping strategy for their own behaviors.

8. If time permits, map a student-generated problem behavior (other than drug use). Then map a positive alternative behavior, emphasizing that the positive alternative leads to better outcomes and that it is important for students to think of realistic positive alternatives that will work for them.

ENDING THE SESSION

1. Have students clarify what they learned.
- Ask students what they found most helpful about mapping an alternative behavior.
- Ask students how they might use the map.

2. Pass out the Session 5 Practice Sheet, Mapping Alternative Behaviors (Reproducible 5-2).
- Tell students they can map past drug use or other problems such as shoplifting, breaking curfew, or arguing with a parent to complete their practice sheets. Make it clear to students that they *should not* engage in drug use in order to complete the practice sheet.
- Remind students that their practice sheets are due at the beginning of the next session, where they will be reviewed in the group.

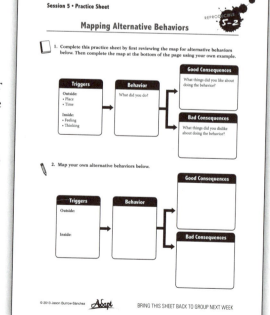

Practice Sheet Icons

Remind students that the book indicates directions they need to read. The pencil indicates they have a writing assignment.

102   Why Do I Do That? Part II

SAMPLE SESSION

SESSION 5

BEGINNING THE SESSION

1 Welcome students.

2 **Review last session's practice sheets.** Discuss two or three student practice sheets.

 Be prepared to spend some time clarifying maps because some students may have found them difficult.

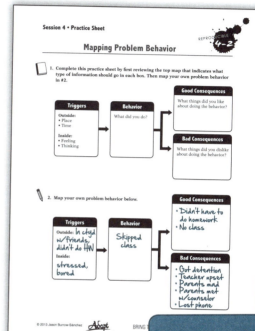

It is great to see everyone today. Please take out your practice sheets. I'm looking forward to seeing how they helped you understand why you engage in certain behaviors—especially problem behaviors. Angie, would you like to start? You can put your practice sheet on the document camera.

Let's start with the behavior. What did you do?
It was a while ago. I skipped class.

What were your triggers? My outside triggers were that I was with friends. We were in the courtyard after lunch. And I didn't do my homework for fifth period. *That's an outside trigger, right?*

Yes, not doing your homework is an outside trigger. It doesn't tell how you felt or what you thought, so it's an outside trigger. I guess that led to feeling a little stressed. And my friends and I were bored. So when my friend asked if I wanted to go to the mall, I thought it sounded good.

Good analysis, Angie. Now, tell us about the consequences. Well, I didn't have to worry about not having my homework. I didn't have to sit through class. And we had fun at the mall.

You identified good consequences—the reasons you left school. What were the bad consequences? I ended up in detention. My teacher was upset. My parents were mad—really mad. They had to come to school and talk to the counselor. And I had to surrender my phone for a month.

Just wondering—now that you've analyzed the problem, your triggers, and the consequences, was it worth it? I guess at the time I thought so, but being without my phone for a month, and all the madness stuff . . . maybe not.

I like seeing how you are able to use the map to understand why you engage in problem behaviors and how the consequences affect you.

The material we cover is the next step—figuring out positive alternative behaviors to serve our needs with better outcomes.

Practice Sheet Completion

- Acknowledge successes—completed practice sheets.
- Address challenges—lost or incomplete practice sheets.
- Summarize steps to successful completion.

ADAPT: Advancing Decision Making and Problem Solving for Teens

SESSION 5

SAMPLE SESSION

PRESENTING THE TOPIC & PRACTICING SKILLS

Mapping Alternative Behaviors

1 **Remind students that the last session focused on understanding *why* people engage in problem behaviors.** This session focuses on selecting positive alternative behaviors that lead to better outcomes.

Last week we talked about why people engage in problem behaviors and the consequences associated with doing so.

This week we are going to map alternative behaviors. Triggers for problem behaviors can become triggers for good behavior. Any questions? Ryan? I don't get that.

Is anyone else confused? OK, let's work through Jordan's example again to see how this works.

2 **Pass out the in-session worksheet, Mapping Alternative Behaviors (Reproducible 5-1).** Then quickly review Jordan's Scenario (or the alternative scenario you used) from Session 4 on the whiteboard.

To review, Jordan smoked marijuana because he felt stressed and mad. After smoking, he felt better temporarily, but he also had an argument with his mom, got grounded, spent the money he was saving for a new skateboard, and didn't do his homework for school. According to his map, Jordan used marijuana to feel better and get rid of angry thoughts, but he also experienced more and longer lasting negative consequences than positive ones.

Any questions about why Jordan smoked marijuana and the outcomes? Jamal? Yeah, I just wouldn't have gotten caught and then all those negatives wouldn't have happened.

I've heard a lot of teens say that. Think about this: How does the strategy of not getting caught usually work out for you? Jamal, how would you answer that? OK, so sometimes it works and sometimes it doesn't.

That's right. It's risky. Here is the question we're going to ask today: If you could do something that provided the same good consequences but that didn't lead to all the bad consequences, would that be something you would consider? I guess so. I'm tired of getting in trouble.

3 **Guide students through another map using skateboarding as the positive alternative behavior.** Fill in each box on the whiteboard. Encourage students to complete their worksheet maps as you discuss the scenario. The completed map will look like Figure 5-1.

Note: The map may seem unrealistic to teens if there are no bad consequences for positive behaviors.

104 Why Do I Do That? Part II

Figure 5-1
Jordan's Alternative Positive Behavior: Skateboarding

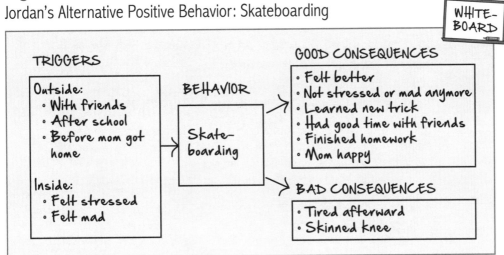

Could Jordan have chosen an alternative behavior that met the same needs as smoking marijuana but led to better outcomes?

Here's what happened. It wasn't long before Jordan was feeling stressed again. He didn't get his homework done and was mad at the same teacher again—same inside triggers as before. He was also with his friends after school. Let's write those down. Maria? His mom was probably not home yet, either.

The triggers are all there. In the past, Jordan would have smoked marijuana. But now he knows the likely consequences. Ryan, did the marijuana help him with his teacher? It's like you said before—he only put off the problem when he smoked marijuana.

Yes, that's a good way to look at it. The marijuana won't help him solve his problem, and it will also lead to bad consequences. Let's stop Jordan right there at the "Behavior" box.

His situation is very similar, but he remembers all of the trouble that smoking marijuana got him into. This time, he remembers that skateboarding makes him feel better. Instead of smoking marijuana, Jordan decided to go skateboarding. Write "skateboarding" in the "Behavior" box on your worksheets.

Skateboarding made Jordan feel better and he wasn't thinking about being mad at his teacher. He learned a new skateboarding trick, fell and skinned his knee, but had a good time with his friends. After skateboarding, he was tired and went home. Jordan's mom was happy with him because he was home on time and finished his homework. What should we write under consequences? Will? He felt better.

Good. Which box—good or bad consequences? Good.

What else? Were there any bad consequences? He skinned his knee . . .

ADAPT: Advancing Decision Making and Problem Solving for Teens

SESSION 5

SAMPLE SESSION

4 **Help students understand two important points about Jordan's alternative behavior:**

1. Jordan experienced more good consequences than bad consequences for skateboarding.

   Now let's look at Jordan's entire map for skateboarding. What do you notice? Maria? He had more good things happen than bad things.

   What do you mean? Well, more good consequences happened from skateboarding than bad consequences. That is the opposite of smoking marijuana—and he didn't spend money, either.

   Excellent observation. I'm glad you noticed that Jordan experienced many more good consequences from skateboarding than he did from smoking marijuana.

2. Skateboarding led to more good consequences *and* served the same need as the problem behavior—it reduced the feeling of being stressed out and mad. Thus, the question becomes, "Why wouldn't you choose the positive alternative?"

   Did Jordan feel less stressed after smoking marijuana? Yes.
   Did Jordan feel less stressed after skateboarding? Yes.

   So, is it fair to say he got the same good consequence from both behaviors? Maria? I don't think so. He didn't feel better for very long when he smoked. He got in trouble right away, but with skateboarding, it was different. He was tired, but it was a good tired. His mom didn't get mad and he got his homework done.

   Is it fair to say skateboarding led to many more good consequences?

   Do you have any questions? Will? He still has to deal with the problem with his teacher.

   You're right, he does. In both examples, he still needs to solve the problem that is making him feel stressed and mad. Do you think he will have a better chance of success with the first or second example? Angie? With skateboarding, he doesn't have to deal with hardly any bad things. He also went home and did his homework. My dad would say he is moving in the right direction.

   Yes, I agree. Dealing with a lot of negative consequences in addition to trying to solve a problem is much tougher.

5 **Have students identify eight to ten other positive alternative behaviors for Jordan.** Write their suggestions on the whiteboard.

If students have difficulty identifying alternative behaviors, have them use the strategies from Session 2—brainstorming, giving yourself advice, thinking about advice from others, and thinking about past problems.

106   *Why Do I Do That? Part II*

SESSION 5

We said that skateboarding is a better option for Jordan than smoking marijuana. Jordan may not be able to skateboard every time he is stressed or angry. Help me figure out some other positive alternatives. Angie? Well, talking to my friends who don't smoke usually works for me.

Great! Jamal? I like to play basketball.

Also great! Ryan? I like to watch sports, so usually I will watch a sports channel until I feel better . . .

 Have students list five positive alternative behaviors they could use for themselves on the backs of their worksheets. Emphasize that choosing a positive alternative is difficult when you're stressed or angry, so they need to create a list of positive alternative behaviors before they actually need one.

Here is an important point about selecting a positive alternative behavior: It is difficult to choose a positive alternative when you are stressed, mad, or upset, so you need to think of positive alternatives before you actually need one. Turn your worksheet over and take a few minutes to list five alternative behaviors you could do instead of using drugs or another problem behavior.

- Have students rank the behaviors on their list from one to five, with one being the most effective alternative.
  Now I want you to order the list from one to five in terms of how effective each behavior would be for you as an alternative to drug use or another problem behavior. Start with one as the most effective and go from there.

- Ask students to post their list where they can see it daily.
  Remember, it is always easier to come up a list of alternative behaviors before you need one. I would like each of you to place your list somewhere you can see it on a daily basis, such as in your notebook, on the wall in your room, or on the inside door of your locker. Seeing the list every day is a good way to remember the alternative behaviors you have available to you.

 Summarize.

- Review Jordan's Scenario. Explain that recognizing triggers (why Jordan smoked marijuana) is an important part of problem solving (finding positive alternative behaviors like skateboarding) that lead to better decisions and outcomes.
  Before we stop today, let's review two important things about Jordan. First, we know why he smoked marijuana—that is, what his triggers were. Second, we know that a positive alternative behavior, skateboarding, helped him feel better and had better outcomes. Understanding why we do things is an important part of making positive changes in our own behavior. It is also important to remember that you have options for alternative behaviors.

ADAPT: Advancing Decision Making and Problem Solving for Teens

- Encourage students to continue thinking about positive alternative behaviors that will work for them.

  Keep thinking about alternative behaviors. It is important to choose ones that will work for you. We know that behaviors that work for some people may not work for others.

- Encourage students to use the mapping strategy for their own behaviors.

  I encourage you to think about using the maps we've learned about to help you figure out your own behaviors. They can help you problem solve and make better decisions. It's important for you to be realistic about your own situation.

 If time permits, map a student-generated problem behavior (other than drug use). Then map a positive alternative behavior, emphasizing that the positive alternative leads to better outcomes and that it is important for students to think of realistic positive alternatives that will work for them.

ENDING THE SESSION

1 Have students clarify what they have learned.
- Ask students what they found most helpful about mapping an alternative behavior.
- Ask students how they might use the map.

  Before we end today, I want to know what you think about mapping alternative behaviors. Specifically, what things do you like about it and what things may be hard to do?

2 Pass out the Session 5 Practice Sheet, Mapping Alternative Behaviors (Reproducible 5-2).

I've handed everyone the Mapping Alternative Behaviors practice sheet. It is similar to the practice sheet from last week but is for an alternative positive behavior. The top part of the page contains an example showing what you need to write in each box of the map. Use this example and the worksheet we did today in group to help you complete your own map.

On the bottom half of the sheet is a blank map for an alternative positive behavior. You can use the map to work on an alternative behavior for the problem behavior that you mapped last week.

Are there any questions?

- Tell students they can map past drug use or other problems such as shoplifting, breaking curfew, or arguing with a parent to complete their practice sheets. Make it clear to students that they *should not* engage in drug use in order to complete the practice sheet. Say something like:

    If you choose to map an alternative behavior to drug use, you can use an example from the past. In other words, you should not use drugs in order to complete this practice sheet.

- Remind students that their practice sheets are due at the beginning of the next session, where they will be reviewed in the group.

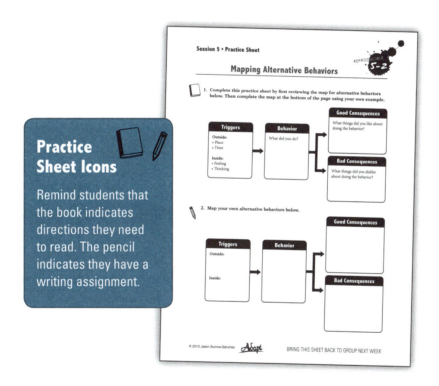

Practice Sheet Icons

Remind students that the book indicates directions they need to read. The pencil indicates they have a writing assignment.

SESSION REFERENCES

Kadden et al., 1992; Meyers & Smith, 1995

WHAT ARE DRUGS AND WHAT DO THEY DO?

SESSION 6

Session Goals

- Students learn about the physical, psychological, and social effects of drug use and how to get accurate information that will help them make informed decisions when offered drugs.
- Students learn the importance of having accurate information in order to make good decisions.
- Students learn to check the accuracy of what they hear or read.

Session Preparation

1. Quickly review the Session Outline.
2. Study the Sample Session and dialogue to help you anticipate how your students might respond to content.
3. Choose to include either Activity 1 (whiteboard activity about negative effects of drugs) or Activity 2 (short true/false quiz) in your session.
4. Complete a Midpoint Progress Report for each student.

Note: You should have a good working knowledge of drug-related information prior to presenting this session. However, you may not know the answers to some questions your students ask. Use this opportunity to model the importance of finding accurate information. You can look up information after the group and share it with students during the next session. To update your own knowledge about drugs and drug use, see *Helping Students Overcome Substance Abuse*, by J. J. Burrow-Sánchez and L. S. Hawken (2007) or the resources listed on Reproducible 6-2.

Materials

- For each student, one copy of:
  - Midpoint Progress Report (Reproducible 6-1)
  - Resources for Drug Information (Reproducible 6-2)
  - **Activity 2 (optional quiz):** Effects of Drugs (Reproducible 6-3). *Note:* If you choose to do this activity orally, you will need only one copy.
  - Session 6 Practice Sheet, Getting Accurate Information About Drugs (Reproducible 6-4)
- Whiteboard and dry-erase markers
- Pencils for students to use during the session

ABOUT THIS SKILL

Most adolescents in the United States will have experimented with at least one drug (usually alcohol) by the time they graduate from high school. Drugs and drug use are provocative topics for teens and are likely to engage them quickly.

Adolescents frequently have misconceptions about the physical, psychological, and social effects of drugs. These misconceptions revolve around misinformation and myths that often come from peers rather than more knowledgeable sources such as teachers, parents, and doctors. Teens may also get conflicting information from friends, parents, teachers, television, and the internet and may not know what to believe.

ADAPT helps students understand this important tenet: Good decisions result in part from having factual information that is relevant to the decision being made.

111

SESSION 6

SESSION OUTLINE

BEGINNING THE SESSION

1 **Welcome students and review last session's practice sheets.** Discuss two or three student practice sheets.

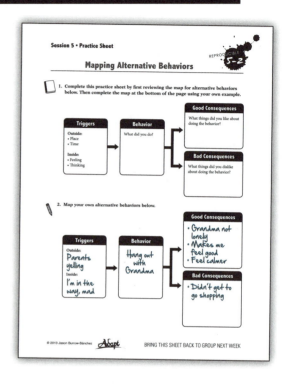

2 **Ask students for feedback on the ADAPT sessions to date.**
- Have students share positive comments and their experiences.
- Have students share concerns and brainstorm solutions.
  Note: Take students' comments seriously as that will increase their ownership of the group.

3 **Hand out Midpoint Progress Reports (Reproducible 6-1).**
- Have students calculate their percentage of completion and identify reasons they have not completed practice sheets.
- Brainstorm strategies for achieving a goal of 80% or higher.

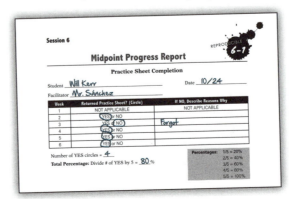

112   *What Are Drugs and What Do They Do?*

PRESENTING THE TOPIC & PRACTICING SKILLS

Accurate Drug Information

1 **Introduce the topic and discuss why it is important to have accurate information about drugs.**

- Share with students that:
  - There are many myths about the physical, psychological, and social effects of drugs.
  - The focus of the session is: What are drugs and what do they do?
  - There are *no* dumb questions.
  - Accurate information is important for making good decisions. Relate the example of buying a car to the decision to use drugs.
- Hand out Resources for Drug Information (Reproducible 6-2), which lists resources that provide accurate information about drugs.

See CD for **Reproducible 6-2**

ADAPT Tip Remind students that everyone has different levels of knowledge about drugs; therefore, it is important that everyone feel comfortable asking questions.

> ### Why You Should Discuss Drugs With Teens
>
> Parents and other adults are sometimes reluctant to discuss drugs because they think bringing up drugs will increase the desire to experiment with them. Teens often have a hard time asking about what they don't know. The result: In the absence of discussions with adults, uninformed adolescents become the experts among their peers and misinformation is often passed along.

2 **Ask students for their questions about drugs and write them on the whiteboard.** Students' questions will help you assess their current knowledge base.

- Go through students' questions and answer them with factual information.
- Tell students that you will use the resources on their handout to research any questions you were unable to answer and share that information during the next session. (See the box on p. 121 for sample questions and responses.)

ADAPT: Advancing Decision Making and Problem Solving for Teens

SESSION OUTLINE

3 **Choose to do either Activity 1 (whiteboard activity about negative drugs effects) or Activity 2 (true/false quiz).**

Activity 1 Instructions

You may need to modify or revise some of the student responses for accuracy, but this activity provides a good opportunity to clarify any misinformation. Make sure to include the negative physical, psychological, and social effects of each drug. In general, teens will have more difficulty identifying the longer-term negative consequences of drug use than more immediate ones.

- Draw a three-column chart on the whiteboard (see Figure 6-1).
- Ask students to help you identify the four most common drugs that teens use. List them in order from most to least common in the "Drugs" column.
- Have students discuss common reasons people use each drug. Write responses in the "Reasons People Use" column.
- Have students discuss negative outcomes that may result from using each drug. Write responses in the "Negative Outcomes" column.

Figure 6-1
Drug information chart

DRUGS	REASONS PEOPLE USE	NEGATIVE OUTCOMES
1. Alcohol	Everyone else does. Easy to get. Makes you feel good.	* Arrested * Doing stupid things * Addicted * Car accidents * Hangover
2. Marijuana	It doesn't hurt anyone. Relaxing.	* Cost * Smell * Arrested
3. Cigarettes	It's cool... Easy to get Habit	* Lung cancer * Cost * Smell * Addicted
4. Inhalants	East to get Feels good	* Might pass out * Headaches * Killing brain cells * Can die from use (sudden sniffing death syndrome, death from huffing)

What Are Drugs and What Do They Do?

Activity 2 Instructions

Challenge common misconceptions students may have about drugs by having them take the true/false quiz Effects of Drugs (Reproducible 6-3).

- Have students take the quiz individually or as a group. If students take the quiz as a group, present the questions orally and have the group decide whether each item is true or false.
- Discuss common misconceptions versus facts for each question or statement. (See the "Drug Facts Versus Myths" box on p. 124 for answers.)

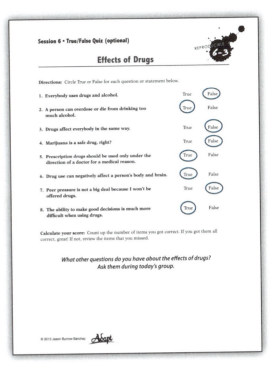

ENDING THE SESSION

1 Have students clarify what they learned about the effects of drugs.

2 Pass out the Session 6 Practice Sheet, Getting Accurate Information About Drugs (Reproducible 6-4).

- Guide students through the activity and ask for questions.
- Remind students that their practice sheets are due at the beginning of the next session, where they will be reviewed in the group.

Practice Sheet Icons

Remind students that the book indicates directions they need to read. The pencil indicates they have a writing assignment.

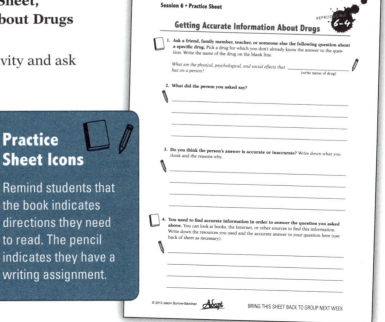

ADAPT: Advancing Decision Making and Problem Solving for Teens

SESSION 6

SAMPLE SESSION

 FACILITATOR Tip If you don't know the answer to a question a student asks about drugs, model the importance of finding accurate information. Tell students you will research the answer and share what you find at the next session.

BEGINNING THE SESSION

1 **Welcome students and review last session's practice sheets.**
Discuss two or three student practice sheets.

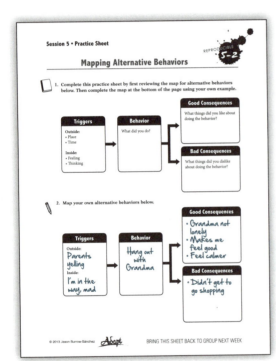

Your task was to use the map to identify alternative positive behaviors you could do instead of using drugs or engaging in other problem behaviors. Who would like to start?

Jamal, would you like to give it a shot? So, here were my outside triggers. Dad was upset. Mom and Dad were yelling. My inside trigger was thinking I was just in the way. And the other inside trigger was getting mad.

Good job identifying your triggers in this situation. What behavior did you identify as a positive option?

I said I could go hang out with my grandma. Sounds kind of weird, but she is always cheerful. We don't talk. We just watch TV or a movie.

So then my consequences were all good. Grandma gets lonely, so I spend time with her. That makes her feel good. It makes me feel good, too. I end up feeling calmer.

You identified positive consequences of hanging out with your grandma. Were there any negative consequences? Well, my dad and I were going to go shopping for a new iPod, but he and my mom got into an argument. If I had hung around, maybe I could have waited out the argument.

Do you think that would have worked? Probably not. It usually makes things worse because I sometimes jump into their arguments, get yelled at, and then get sent to my bedroom. That's usually when I get so mad that I sneak out and drink or something.

Okay, so hanging out with your grandma led to many more positive consequences than negative consequences. Yeah, it did.

Hanging out with your grandma also provided you with an alternative positive behavior to jumping into the argument your parents were having. Yeah.

This is a great example of using an alternative positive behavior. Do you think the mapping exercise will help you in the future? Yeah, it makes me think about triggers and stuff . . .

What Are Drugs and What Do They Do?

You all came up with alternative behaviors to drug use or positive options to problems. Understanding why you do certain things is an important part of making better decisions. I hope this will help you stop and think when you encounter a problem. You always have options.

2 Ask students for feedback on the ADAPT sessions to date.

- Have students share positive comments and their experiences.
  Today is the halfway point for ADAPT. This is a good time to find out how things have been going these past six weeks. What are some of the things you like about the program? Will? I'm glad you don't make me talk. *OK. I'm glad you are still coming. Are your practice sheets interesting?* Yeah, they're OK.

- Have students share concerns and brainstorm solutions.
  Note: Take students' comments seriously as that will increase their ownership of the group.
  What are some of the things we could do better in the remaining six weeks? Maria? Well, I think it would be better if we all talked. *That's fair.*

  What does anyone else think? Angie? I don't think we should make anyone talk. That isn't fair, either.

  Let's brainstorm ideas for encouraging people to talk without making them feel uncomfortable. Megan? I think we should . . .

  You all came up with some good ideas. Let's do this. I'll try to encourage each of you to participate, but you have the option to just say "pass" if you are feeling uncomfortable. Does that work?

3 Hand out Midpoint Progress Reports (Reproducible 6-1).

Our goal is to have everyone in the group complete at least 80% of the practice sheets by the end of the program. The practice sheets are important because they give you the chance to practice and use the tools we've worked on in your own lives. I'm passing out a piece of paper with your name on it and the number of practice sheets you have completed up through week 5.

- Have students calculate their percentage of completion and identify reasons they have not completed practice sheets.
- Brainstorm strategies for achieving a goal of 80% or higher.
  If you are at or above 80%, raise your hand. Great job! I'm sure you can all get there. What are some of the things that have prevented you from completing the practice sheets? Forgetting, losing it, not getting around to it . . .

  Let's brainstorm things that would help.

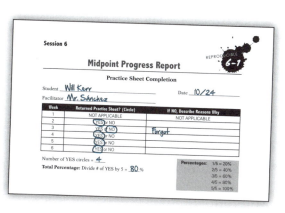

SESSION 6

SAMPLE SESSION

PRESENTING THE TOPIC & PRACTICING SKILLS

Accurate Drug Information

> **Why You Should Discuss Drugs**
>
> Parents and other adults are sometimes reluctant to discuss drugs because they think bringing up drugs will increase the desire to experiment with them. Teens often have a hard time asking about what they don't know. The result: In the absence of discussions with adults, uninformed adolescents become the experts among their peers and misinformation is often passed along.

1 **Introduce the topic and discuss why it is important to have accurate information about drugs.**

This week we are going to talk about what drugs are and the physical, psychological, and social effects they have. Teens usually have many questions about drugs but frequently don't get accurate information about them.

- Share with students that:
  - There are many myths about the physical, psychological, and social effects of drugs.

    Usually, we learn about drugs from our friends, family, teachers, and television. We rarely check out the information to determine if it is accurate. Unfortunately, not all of the information we receive is accurate.

  - The focus of the session is: What are drugs and what do they do?

    Most teens are offered drugs at some point before they graduate from high school. That's a fact. We also know it is hard to make good decisions if you don't have accurate information. So, this week we are answering the question, "What are drugs and what do they do?"

  - There are *no* dumb questions.

    Remember, there are no dumb questions, so I hope you feel comfortable asking anything. We have worked on effective tools for problem solving and decision making. Today, our goal is to add accurate information about drugs to your toolbox.

ADAPT Tip   Remind students that everyone has different levels of knowledge about drugs; so, it is important that everyone feel comfortable asking questions.

> Teens often have a lot of questions about alcohol and drugs, but they don't always know where to go for reliable information. Some teens have a hard time asking about what they don't know and rely on information from others.

- Accurate information is important for making good decisions. Relate the example of buying a car to the decision to use drugs.

  Some teens think, "Who cares about accurate information?" To answer that, let's compare using drugs with buying a car. Imagine you are going to buy a car with your hard-earned money. What would you do before buying the car? Ryan? I'd want a good buy.

  How could Ryan find a good buy? Maria? My mom always looks at Consumer Reports *before she buys something.*

  Ryan could find information by doing research online or in some sort of a consumer's report. Maria, do you know why she checks Consumer Reports. Yes. She says she doesn't trust ads.

118   *What Are Drugs and What Do They Do?*

Your mom would suggest going to what we call an independent source—one that is based on fact, not opinion. Yes.

Jamal, what would you do if you were going to buy a car? I'd ask my uncle for help. *Why is that?* He's a mechanic.

Great, so you would go to an expert. What else?

You've come up with a great list of ways you would research what kind of car to buy. You would look at multiple sources. You would look at sources that are based on fact or that are truthful. And you would evaluate information or fact check.

In other words, you would do your homework. Do you think that would help you get a good buy and avoid a clunker?

Accurate information helps people make better decisions. Here is my question: If you think it is a good idea to do your homework on buying a car, wouldn't you also want to get accurate information about things you take, specifically drugs? Especially when the consequences of taking drugs can be much more negative than buying a clunker.

- Hand out Resources for Drug Information (Reproducible 6-2), which lists resources that provide accurate information about drugs.

Selecting an Example

Older teens often relate to a car-buying example. For younger students, you may wish to substitute buying a cell phone, video game, or iPod.

See CD for **Reproducible 6-2**

2 Ask students for their questions about drugs and write them on the whiteboard. Students' questions will help you assess their current knowledge base.

ADAPT Tip

Many teens want accurate information about drugs. Students often report that the only message they receive at school is "Just don't do drugs!" They also report that this message is not very helpful. Therefore, it is important to remind students that this is their opportunity to ask questions about drugs so they can make decisions based on accurate information.

You probably get a lot of information about drugs from your friends, older siblings, school, television, movies, the Internet, and other places.

One of our goals today is to obtain accurate information about drugs. A good way to do that is to ask questions. This is your opportunity to ask anything you want to know about drugs.

Remember, there are no dumb questions. If you have a question, someone else may have the same question. As you ask questions, I will write them on the board and then we'll go through them. If I don't have an answer, I'll do some research and tell you the answers next week. What questions do you have?

ADAPT: Advancing Decision Making and Problem Solving for Teens

SESSION 6

SAMPLE SESSION

 ADAPT Tip Write down the questions students have about drugs for future reference. You can use these questions in future ADAPT groups that you facilitate.

- Go through students' questions and answer them with factual information. See the next page for sample questions and responses.
- Tell students that you will use the resources on their handout to research any questions you were unable to answer and share that information during the next session.

3 Choose to do either Activity 1 (whiteboard activity about negative drugs effects) or Activity 2 (true/false quiz).

Activity 1 Instructions

You may need to modify or revise some of the student responses for accuracy, but this exercise is a good opportunity to clarify any misinformation. Make sure to include the negative physical, psychological, and social effects of each drug. In general, teens will have more difficulty identifying the long-term negative consequences of drug use than more immediate ones.

- Draw a three-column chart on the board (see Figure 6-1 on p. 122).
- Ask students to help you identify the four most common drugs that teens use. List them in order from most to least common in the "Drugs" column.

I have drawn a table on the board with three columns labeled "Drugs," "Reasons People Use," and "Negative Outcomes." Many teens have questions about why people use drugs and the negative physical, psychological, and social effects drugs can have. Unfortunately, many teens don't ask questions about drugs because they don't want to appear dumb in front of their friends. Today, we are going to list some drugs, discuss why people use them, and consider the negative effects they can have.

Help me list, in order, the four most common drugs that teens use. I will write them in the first column. What drug should we list first?

- Have students discuss common reasons people use each drug. Write responses in the "Reasons People Use" column.

Now I want you to help me come up with common reasons why people use each of these drugs. Let's start with the first drug.

What Are Drugs and What Do They Do?

COMMON QUESTIONS ABOUT DRUGS

Your students' questions will help you and them understand what they know and don't know about the effects of drugs. Their questions will allow you to engage them in a thoughtful discussion.

Common questions and possible responses follow. Global responses to questions (for example, "Alcohol does bad things to the body") will not satisfy students' curiosity. Be prepared with fairly detailed answers.

1 *Why do people take drugs?*

General response: When teens are offered drugs, they often feel peer pressure to use the drug.

People often continue taking a drug because it alters the way they think or feel. For example, a person may take a drug to escape or avoid negative feelings caused by a problem. Unfortunately, the drugs don't make the problem(s) go away.

2 *What is a drug?*

General response: For purposes of ADAPT, a drug is something that people take to change the way they think or feel.

3 *Do all drugs harm you?*

General response: Any drug can have negative physical, psychological, and social effects, but the specific effects will depend on the type of drug.

4 *I heard prescription drugs are not harmful because they are prescribed by doctors. Is that true?*

General response: That is not true. Prescription drugs are prescribed by doctors to help people. However, when people take a prescription drug that is not prescribed for them by a doctor, the drug can be very harmful.

5 *I heard that marijuana is not really a drug. Is that true?*

General response: Let's go back to our definition of what a drug is and answer the following question: "Is marijuana something that is used to change the way a person thinks or feels?" I would say the answer is most definitely "yes." So marijuana is definitely a drug.

6 *I heard marijuana (or another drug) is safe. Is that true?*

General response: There are no safe drugs, and all drugs can have negative physical, psychological, and social effects. In fact, marijuana use has been linked to breathing problems, difficulty learning and remembering information, and a general lack of motivation for doing things.

7 *I heard using drugs right before taking an exam (for example, marijuana or Ritalin) will help you do better on the exam. Is that true?*

General response: There is no evidence that taking drugs before an exam will help you do better. In fact, you will likely do worse because the drug will negatively affect your performance. The exception is a student who is actually being treated for ADHD by a doctor and taking medication as prescribed. In that case, the medication will help him or her maintain attention and focus on the exam.

8 *I heard heroin (or another drug) is dangerous. Is that true?*

General response: All drugs can have negative physical, psychological, and social effects, so I would consider any drug to be potentially dangerous. A drug like heroin is especially dangerous because it is highly addictive and is typically injected into a vein with a syringe. This can lead to infections at the injection site and the increased possibility of contracting a disease like HIV/AIDS from sharing dirty needles.

ADAPT: Advancing Decision Making and Problem Solving for Teens

SESSION 6

SAMPLE SESSION

- Have students discuss negative outcomes that may result from using each drug. Write responses in the "Negative Outcomes" column.

  Now I want you to help me complete the last column in the table by coming up with the most common negative effects—physical, psychological, and social effects—each drug can have. We can think about things that happen right away and things that may occur years later. For example, a negative effect of smoking cigarettes may be lung cancer. That negative effect is very real and deadly, but it may take years before you get the disease.

Figure 6-1
Drug information chart

WHITE-BOARD

DRUGS	REASONS PEOPLE USE	NEGATIVE OUTCOMES
1. Alcohol	Everyone else does. Easy to get. Makes you feel good.	* Arrested * Doing stupid things * Addicted * Car accidents * Hangover
2. Marijuana	It doesn't hurt anyone. Relaxing.	* Cost * Smell * Arrested
3. Cigarettes	It's cool... Easy to get Habit	* Lung cancer * Cost * Smell * Addicted
4. Inhalants	Easy to get Feels good	* Might pass out * Headaches * Killing brain cells * Can die from use (sudden sniffing death syndrome, death from huffing)

What Are Drugs and What Do They Do?

SESSION 6

Activity 2 Instructions

Challenge common misconceptions students may have about drugs by having them take the true/false quiz, Effects of Drugs (Reproducible 6-3).

It is common for teens to have misconceptions about drugs, and this is usually because they don't have accurate information. To demonstrate this point, we are going to take a quiz.

ADAPT Tip: Students may groan, but stay positive!

> **Prevalence Statistics**
>
> Your school or district may have drug-use statistics that provide more accurate estimates for your setting.
>
> You can find national prevalence rates from the resources listed on the Resources for Drug Information handout (Reproducible 6-2). Government or school organizations in many states provide state-specific rates of drug use.

- Have students take the quiz individually or as a group. Use the format that best fits your group. If students take the quiz as a group, present the questions orally and have the group decide whether each item is true or false.

  Oral Quiz Option
  I know what you're thinking: Why do we have to take a quiz? This is a fun quiz. I am going to read some questions or statements, and the group can decide if they are true or false by majority rule. Then we can discuss why the question is true or false. OK, let's get started.

  Written Quiz Option
  I know what you're thinking: Why do we have to take a quiz? This is a short, fun quiz. Circle True or False for each statement. I'll give you a few minutes to do this, and then we can discuss the reasons why the statement is true or false. Let's get started.

- Discuss common misconceptions versus facts for each question or statement. (See the "Drug Facts Versus Myths" box on the following page for answers.)

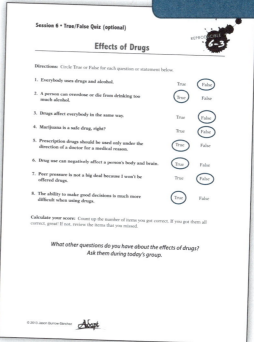

ADAPT: Advancing Decision Making and Problem Solving for Teens   123

SESSION 6

SAMPLE SESSION

DRUG FACTS VERSUS MYTHS

Try to make the quiz relevant to your students by anticipating questions students in your group may ask about drugs.

1. Everybody uses drugs and alcohol.

False: Research indicates that teens commonly overestimate peer drug use. Teens often justify their own drug use by saying things like: "At least I'm not using as much as most other teens my age" or "A lot of people do it—it's no big deal."

2. A person can overdose or die from drinking too much alcohol.

True: Alcohol is a drug classified as a depressant. Depressants are types of drugs that decrease activity in the central nervous system (CNS) when taken. The CNS controls things in the body such as brain activity, breathing, and heart rate. Taking too much of a depressant can cause a person to lose consciousness and eventually die because of decreased activity in the central nervous system. This is referred to as alcohol poisoning and is generally influenced by such factors as the amount a person drinks, their muscle to fat ratio, and when their last meal was eaten. Mixing alcohol with other depressants, such as downers, pain medication, and tranquilizers, is especially dangerous because the negative effects become intensified.

3. Drugs affect everybody in the same way.

False: Teens commonly think that watching how others respond to a drug predicts how they will respond. This is a misperception. Two people can react very differently after using the same drug. The specific reaction depends on factors such as amount of the drug taken, prior experience with the drug, and body chemistry.

Teens can expect that being under the influence of drugs will decrease their ability to make good decisions and problem solve. Drugs generally decrease a person's inhibitions, so people often do things under the influence of drugs that they normally would not do.

4. Marijuana is a safe drug, right?

False: Teens commonly think that some drugs are safe while others are not. However, there are no safe drugs because all drugs have some level of danger. For example, marijuana has been linked to problems with balance and coordination, learning and memory, frequent coughs, respiratory infections, and lowered motivation to do important activities such as school, work, and sports. In fact, marijuana smoke contains more carcinogens than tobacco smoke and is related to many crimes, such as possession, selling, and stealing to buy it.

5. Prescription drugs should be used only under the direction of a doctor for a medical reason.

True: Teens have a common misperception that prescription drugs are safe because they are prescribed by doctors. Teens who abuse prescription medication do so while not under the direction of a doctor, which can be very dangerous. Prescription medications should be used only by the person they are prescribed for and under the direction of a doctor.

6. Drug use can negatively affect a person's body and brain.

True: Drugs work by changing the levels of chemical messengers, called neurotransmitters, in the brain. Scientists know that human brains don't fully develop until the mid-20s. These two factors put teens at high risk for negatively affecting the normal development of their brain if they are using drugs. The negative developmental impact on the brain from teen drug use depends on things like what drug is used, how much, and for how long. The age a person starts using a drug, as well as a person's own brain chemistry, makes a difference. Scientists have found that the brains of people who started using drugs as children differ in size and in the way they function from the brains of people who did not grow up using drugs.

7. Peer pressure is not a big deal because I won't be offered drugs.

False: Teens are commonly first offered drugs from other teens. Thus, peer pressure is a big deal and will likely influence a person's decision to use drugs if they are offered. Thinking about ways to refuse drugs when offered is the focus of the next group session.

8. The ability to make good decisions is much more difficult when using drugs.

True: Teens don't usually realize how much their decision-making and problem-solving capacity is diminished when they are under the influence of drugs. In general, people usually make poorer decisions (that usually lead to more problems) when under the influence of drugs. The first good decision to make is to not use drugs!

What Are Drugs and What Do They Do?

SESSION 6

ENDING THE SESSION

1 **Have students clarify what they learned about the effects of drugs.**

Before we end today, I want to know what you thought about the information we learned today. Specifically, what things were new to you and what things did you already know?

2 **Pass out the Session 6 Practice Sheet, Getting Accurate Information About Drugs (Reproducible 6-4).**

- Guide students through the activity and ask for questions.

  I've handed everyone a practice sheet entitled "Getting Accurate Information about Drugs." This sheet asks you to work through a few steps to obtain accurate information about drugs from another person.

  First, you need to ask someone such as a friend, family member, or teacher the following question: "What physical, psychological, and social effects does [name of drug] have on a person?" You can pick the drug that you include in the question.

  Next, you need to write down what the person said.

  Then think about what the person said and decide whether you think the information is accurate or not.

  Finally, you need to do some research to determine the correct answers to your question. Use the resources for finding accurate information about drugs I handed out earlier. Are there any questions?

- Remind students that their practice sheets are due at the beginning of the next session, where they will be reviewed in the group.

  Great, I look forward to reviewing these with you next week. Have a great week!

Practice Sheet Icons

Remind students that the book indicates directions they need to read. The pencil indicates they have a writing assignment.

SESSION REFERENCES

Burrow-Sánchez & Hawken, 2007.
National Institute on Drug Abuse, 2011.

ADAPT: Advancing Decision Making and Problem Solving for Teens

HOW DO I REFUSE DRUGS?
Triggers, Communication, Reasons

Session Goals

- Students learn effective drug refusal skills.
- Students learn how peer pressure influences their decisions about drug use.
- Students learn that having personal reasons for not using drugs makes it easier to refuse drugs.

Session Preparation

1. Quickly review the Session Outline.
2. Study the Sample Session and sample dialogue to help you anticipate how your students might respond to content.
3. Display the Communicate "No" Effectively poster (Reproducible 7-1) or copy on the whiteboard.

Materials

- Presentation copy of Communicate "No" Effectively poster (Reproducible 7-1)
  Note: Project on a document camera or enlarge (129% on 11" x 17" paper).
- For each student, one copy of:
  - Triggers, Communication, Reasons (Reproducible 7-2)
  - Session 7 Practice Sheet, Effectively Refusing Drugs (Reproducible 7-3)
- Whiteboard and dry-erase markers
- Pencils for students to use during the session

ABOUT THIS SKILL

Teens need to learn effective skills for refusing drugs that they can generalize across people, places, and situations. It is important for teens to practice drug refusal skills and have a commitment to not use drugs prior to being offered drugs.

SESSION 7 — SESSION OUTLINE

BEGINNING THE SESSION

1. Welcome students.

2. Review last session's practice sheets. Discuss two or three student practice sheets.

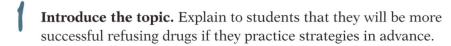

PRESENTING THE TOPIC & PRACTICING SKILLS

Drug Refusal Skills

1. Introduce the topic. Explain to students that they will be more successful refusing drugs if they practice strategies in advance.

2. Pass out Triggers, Communication, Reasons (Reproducible 7-2). On the whiteboard, write the three key words for remembering how to effectively refuse drugs: Triggers, Communication, Reasons.

STEP 1: Triggers. Know your triggers for drug use.

ADAPT Tip: When discussing triggers, make connections with mapping problem behaviors and mapping alternative behaviors.

- Discuss the *people* who make it more difficult to refuse drugs. Understanding peer pressure enhances students' ability to refuse drugs. Have students define peer pressure and share examples from their own experience.
- To combat peer pressure, have the students imagine the following scenario: If you asked your friend to take the bad consequences of drug use for you, what do you think your friend would say?

128 How Do I Refuse Drugs?

Note: This question often generates some laughs from students. Use humor to illustrate to students that they will suffer the consequences of drug use, not the person who offered them drugs.
- Help students understand that people they have used drugs with in the past are triggers. Then have them complete 1A on the worksheet.
- Discuss *situations* or *places* that make it more difficult to refuse drugs, then have students complete 1B on the worksheet.
- Discuss the *types of drugs* that are difficult to refuse, and have students complete 1C on the worksheet.

STEP 2: Communication. Communicate "no" effectively. Teach students how to effectively communicate their decision not to use drugs. *Note*: Use Reproducible 7-1 as a visual aid.

- Respond quickly.
- Start with the word "no." Then do one or more of the following:
  - Suggest doing something else.
  - Mention the negative consequences.
  - Ask not to be offered drugs.
  - Say that being asked to use drugs makes you uncomfortable.
- Make sure that what you say matches how you say it.

STEP 3: Reasons. Know your personal reasons for not using drugs. Help students develop their own reasons for not using drugs and have them write their reasons as goals to achieve on their worksheets. *Note*: If students have personal reasons for not using drugs, refusing drugs will be easier.

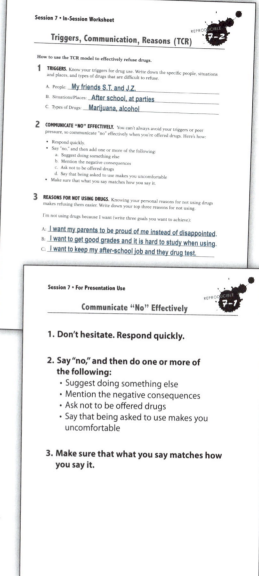

3 Summarize.

- The first word to remember is *triggers*. Know your triggers.
- The next word to remember is *communication*. Communicate "no" effectively.
- The third word to remember is *reasons*. Remember your personal reasons for not using drugs.
- Use drug refusal skills in ways that work for you.

ADAPT: Advancing Decision Making and Problem Solving for Teens

SESSION OUTLINE

4 **Guide students through the Drug Refusal Role-Play.** Start by drawing the following table on the whiteboard:

SCENARIO	PEOPLE	PLACES/SITUATIONS	DRUG
1	M, R, O	Park, O's house	Alcohol
2			
3			

The Drug Refusal Role-Play:

1. Ask a student to generate a scenario by filling in the table.
2. Have the student role-play refusing drugs using the scenario. Discuss with the group.
3. If the student needs help, ask the group for suggestions.
4. Repeat with other students as time permits.

ENDING THE SESSION

1 **Have students clarify what they learned.**

Ask students what they found most helpful about drug refusal skills and how they might use the skills.

2 **Pass out the Session 7 Practice Sheet, Effectively Refusing Drugs (Reproducible 7-3).**

- Walk students through the practice sheet.
- Remind students to use past examples or imagine what they would do in certain situations to complete the practice sheet.
- Remind students that their practice sheets are due at the beginning of the next session, where they will be reviewed in the group.

Practice Sheet Icons

Remind students that the book indicates directions they need to read. The pencil indicates they have a writing assignment.

---

130   How Do I Refuse Drugs?

SAMPLE SESSION

SESSION 7

BEGINNING THE SESSION

1 Welcome students.

2 **Review last session's practice sheets.** Discuss two or three student practice sheets.

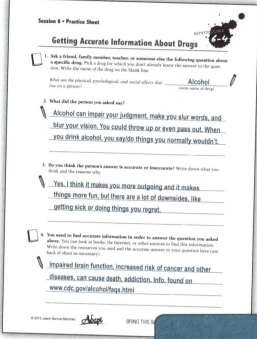

PRESENTING THE TOPIC & PRACTICING SKILLS

Drug Refusal Skills

1 **Introduce the topic.** Explain to students that they will be more successful refusing drugs if they practice strategies in advance.

Last week we talked about the effects that drugs have on us. This week we are going to learn how to effectively refuse drugs.

You've probably heard the message "Just say NO!" Unfortunately, it's not always as easy as that.

Today, we are going to think about how to refuse drugs before you are in a situation where you are asked to take drugs. Practicing strategies in advance will help you be more successful.

2 **Pass out Triggers, Communication, Reasons (Reproducible 7-2).** On the whiteboard, write the three key words for remembering how to effectively refuse drugs: Triggers, Communication, Reasons.

We're going to learn three steps for effectively refusing drugs. The steps involve the key words on the board: Triggers, Communication, and Reasons. This worksheet will help you remember those words and the related steps to effectively refusing drugs.

Practice Sheet Completion

- Acknowledge successes—completed practice sheets.
- Address challenges—lost or incomplete practice sheets.
- Summarize steps to successful completion.

ADAPT: Advancing Decision Making and Problem Solving for Teens   131

SESSION 7

SAMPLE SESSION

 ADAPT Tip When discussing triggers, make connections with mapping problem behaviors and mapping alternative behaviors.

STEP 1: Triggers. Know your triggers for drug use.

When we worked on mapping problem behaviors and mapping alternative behaviors, we looked at triggers.

The first step in effectively refusing drugs is to identify your triggers. A trigger for drug use is a person, place, situation, or type of drug that makes it more difficult for you to refuse. If you know your triggers before you encounter them, it will increase your chances of successfully refusing drugs.

- Discuss the *people* who make it more difficult to refuse drugs. Understanding peer pressure enhances students' ability to refuse drugs. Have students define peer pressure and share examples from their own experience.

Before moving on to more triggers, let's talk about peer pressure. Many teens underestimate the power of peer pressure.

Who can explain what peer pressure is? Megan? It's when friends pressure you to do something. Can you be more specific? It would be like a friend asking you to smoke marijuana, but you don't want to. Your friend really wants you to, so you do.

But why do you do it? Because you don't want to disappoint your friends, or they make fun of you for not smoking.

It sounds like you are concerned about the negative reaction your friends may have if you say you don't want to smoke. Yeah, exactly.

Does that make sense to others in the group? Does that really happen? Maria? Yeah, definitely—it happens all the time.

Jamal, looks like you don't agree. I don't really think it happens to me. Why not? I make my own decisions. Nobody tells me what to do.

Angie, you don't look convinced. It happens to him, too. Guys just have a harder time admitting it. (Group, including Jamal, laughs.)

It sounds like most of you have experienced peer pressure—friends wanting you to do something you don't want to do. Who can give us a personal example of peer pressure to use drugs? Angie? Last week, my friend asked me to walk across the street during lunch and smoke a cigarette with her. I really didn't want to leave campus or smoke a cigarette. I really don't like smoking cigarettes at all, but I ended up smoking with her anyway.

Can you tell us why you ended up smoking even though you didn't want to? I felt like she would be mad at me or think less of me. It sounds kind of stupid now, but it didn't seem that way then.

How Do I Refuse Drugs?

What you are describing is really normal. Teens often find themselves doing things they don't really want to because of the pressure they get from other teens. Afterwards, they can see it more clearly and are often disappointed in themselves. In the moment, it's not always easy to see.

Friends may ask you to use drugs because: 1) they don't want to use by themselves—using with another person makes them feel better about using, and 2) some of your friends may not care about your personal goals about not using drugs or the negative consequences that you may experience from using drugs—at least, not the friends who offer you drugs.

Maria, you look like you're not buying this. Well, I think my friends care about what happens to me.

OK, let me be more specific. When friends offer you drugs, they are not usually considering the bad consequences that you could experience as a result of using. Can you see that? Yes, I guess so.

- To combat peer pressure, have the students imagine the following scenario: If you asked your friend to take the bad consequences of drug use for you, what do you think your friend would say?

  Ask yourself this question: If I use drugs, will my friend take the consequences if I get caught?

  In other words, you say to your friend, "Hey, you offered me marijuana. If I smoke with you, I will get in big trouble with my folks. Will you take the bad consequences for me?" What do you think your friend would say?

  Note: This question often generates some laughs from students. Use humor to illustrate to students that they will suffer the consequences of drug use, not the person who offered them drugs.

  OK, I see your point.

  Regardless of what type of friend offers you drugs, you are the one who will have to deal with any negative consequences.

- Help students understand that people they have used drugs with in the past are triggers. Then have them complete 1A on the worksheet.

  If you've used drugs with people in the past, they will be triggers for future drug use. Think about the people you're most likely to use drugs with. These people are your triggers. On your worksheet, write down the initials of people you're most likely to do drugs with.

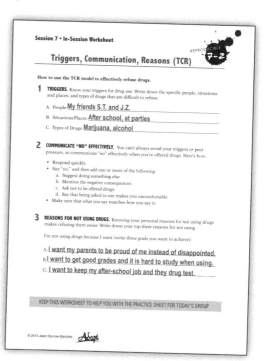

ADAPT: Advancing Decision Making and Problem Solving for Teens 133

SESSION 7

SAMPLE SESSION

- Discuss *situations* or *places* that make it more difficult to refuse drugs, then have students complete 1B on the worksheet.

  There are many situations or places where you may be offered drugs, such as at a party, at school, after school, at a friend's house, and so on. Are there any places that I missed?

  These situations or places are also triggers. Is it harder to refuse drugs at a party than at school? At a party, obviously . . .

  Good. Being at a party is a higher risk situation than being at school. What are high-risk situations or places for you? Angie? Well, being at one friend's house is really hard because I always know she will ask me if I want to use.

  Good for you to know. Ryan? At parties, there's always drugs being offered . . .

  Thanks for sharing those examples. If you can identify situations or places that are triggers, you will be more successful at refusing drugs. Go ahead and fill in 1B on your worksheet.

- Discuss the *types of drugs* that are difficult to refuse, then have students complete 1C on the worksheet.

  Generally, teens find that they have more difficulty refusing some drugs than others. For example, it may be more difficult to refuse marijuana than alcohol. Does this make sense to you? Does anyone have examples of this? Megan? It's easy for me to refuse alcohol because I really don't like the way it tastes, but it's usually tougher for me to refuse marijuana.

  Thanks for sharing that example. There are many reasons why it may be more difficult to refuse certain drugs. In general, drugs that you've used more often are harder to refuse. Your past experience with a drug influences your future behavior with that drug. For example, you may have more experience using marijuana than cocaine. In general, this makes marijuana harder to refuse when offered; however, cocaine is a drug that is highly addictive and it doesn't take long to become addicted to it. So, in part, this will also depend on the specific drug.

  Our past experience with a drug produces powerful cues that influence what we will do the next time we encounter that drug. These cues are similar to the triggers that we discussed with mapping problem behaviors. Drug cues or triggers include things like locations where you've used, people you've used with, and paraphernalia—pipes, lighters, and so on—associated with using. These cues produce mental and physical reactions in our body that can be difficult to ignore. The longer a person uses a drug, generally the cues become stronger and harder to ignore. Does anyone have experience with cues for certain drugs? Ryan? Yeah, like when I'm at my friend's house. He has a lot of stuff in his room that reminds me of using marijuana—pipes, stuff like that. Even the smell of his room reminds me of using.

  So, when you experience these things, what happens? I think about using.

134   *How Do I Refuse Drugs?*

What if you don't want to use? That's tough. Like the smell is inviting me to light up.

What could you do if you don't want to use? Well, I usually avoid going to that friend's house because I don't want to be tempted.

Yes, that sounds like a good idea. You have described one of your triggers.

STEP 2: Communication. Communicate "no" effectively. Teach students how to effectively communicate their decision not to use drugs. *Note*: Use Reproducible 7-1 as a visual aid.

A simple way to lower your risk is to avoid specific people and certain situations or places that you have identified as triggers for drug use. Ryan, what do you think? That sounds great, but there is no way to always avoid those things. You would have to lock yourself up in your room and never come out.

That is funny. You are right. We cannot always avoid things that are triggers for us. Sometimes we can, but sometimes we can't. So we need to have skills to use when we encounter our triggers. Let's start discussing some of the skills we will need in those situations.

We are going to discuss how to say "no" so the other person understands that you mean it. An effective "no" is your best defense against peer pressure. Here are the steps to saying "no" effectively.

- Respond quickly.

    First, respond quickly. The longer you wait, the more likely the other person is to keep pressuring you.

- Start with the word "no."

    Second, your response should start with the word "no," leaving the other person with no confusion about your decision.

    Then do one or more of the following:

    a. Suggest doing something else.

       Then say something else to get your message across. Examples include suggesting to the person that you both do something else, like skateboarding or hanging out with a friend who does not use. You could say something like, "No, but why don't we go skateboarding instead?" or "No, but let's go over to Parker's house and see what he is doing." What other activities could you see yourself suggesting in a situation like this? Ryan? I usually just tell the person that I will get in trouble for using. So go ask someone else.

       That's a good response and leads to our next set of examples.

SAMPLE SESSION

  b. Mention the negative consequences.

  You could also mention potential negative consequences or provide a realistic excuse. You could say something like:
  - *No, my mom will be all over me if she catches me using.*
  - *No, my probation officer drug tests me and I can't come up positive for anything.*
  - *No. I really need to finish my homework, and that won't help me do that.*

  What do you think about those things? Maria? It's easier when the other person knows why you don't want to use. It seems like that takes the pressure off. But sometimes they will keep asking.
  Right. In those situations you may have to be even more direct.

  c. Ask not to be offered drugs.

  Ask the person not to offer you drugs. For example, you could say something like "I'm trying not to use. Please don't offer it to me." Remember, real friends will be supportive of your decision not to use. Will, what do you think? Sure.

  Jamal? Yeah, I can do that. It may be hard at first, but you're right, a friend doesn't really want you to get in trouble.

  d. Tell the person that being asked to use drugs makes you feel uncomfortable.

  You can tell the person who is asking you to use drugs that it makes you uncomfortable. For example, you could say, "No, and you are really making me uncomfortable by offering me marijuana, so please stop." Angie, any thoughts? I actually like that one because it kind of throws them off. They will probably be like "What?" and not know what to say.

- Make sure that what you say matches how you say it.

  Let's talk a little about body language and voice. If a person says, "I'm fine," but is slouching and not looking at you, there's a mismatch.

  If a person says, "Yes, I totally believe you," but rolls his eyes, that's a mismatch.

  If you are refusing drugs, make sure <u>what</u> you are saying matches how you say it. When you say "no" to drugs, your voice should be clear, your body posture should be confident, and you should look the person in the eyes. These things will help the other person know that you are serious about your decision not to use drugs.

STEP 3: Reasons. Know your personal reasons for not using drugs. Help students develop their own reasons for not using drugs and have them write their reasons as goals to achieve on their worksheets.
Note: If students have personal reasons for not using drugs, refusing drugs will be easier.

In addition to being an effective communicator, it is important for you to know your personal reasons for not using drugs. Personal reasons are like goals. They are

How Do I Refuse Drugs?

things you are trying to accomplish or "stick to" because they are important to you. In general, when someone can identify a personal reason for doing something, it increases their ability to stick with their goal.

Some examples of goals are:
- *I'm not using drugs because I want to graduate.*
- *I'm not using drugs because I want to do better in school,*
- *I'm not using drugs because I want to get off probation.*
Now I want each of you to write down your personal reasons on the worksheet.

Angie, what is one thing you wrote down? Well, I'm not doing drugs because I want to do better in school. I promised my mom I'd do better. When I'm high, I can't do my homework.

Good. What about you, Jamal? I want to go out for football this year, but this school does random drug testing for athletes. If I come up dirty, I won't be able to play. I've seen this happen to other people, and I don't want it to happen to me.

Thanks, Angie and Jamal. Knowing your personal reasons for not using drugs will be helpful when you encounter high-risk situations.

3 Summarize.

- ### The first word to remember is *triggers*. Know your triggers.
  As we discussed an important part of refusing drugs is to be aware of your triggers—people, situations and places, and types of drugs.

  Don't underestimate the power of peer pressure. Peer pressure is more powerful than most teens realize. The easiest solution to peer pressure is to avoid people who are your triggers for using. Of course, that doesn't always work!

- ### The next word to remember is *communication*. Communicate "no" effectively.
  When you find yourself confronted by your triggers, you need to use effective communication skills. This includes practicing things like: saying "no" right away, suggesting doing something else, mentioning the negative consequences, asking not to be offered drugs, explaining that being asked makes you uncomfortable, and making sure that what you say matches your voice and body language.

- ### The third word to remember is *reasons*. Remember your personal reasons for not using drugs.
  I encourage you to keep reminding yourself of your personal reasons for not using drugs. Knowing your reasons will strengthen your commitment to not use.

- ### Use drug refusal skills in ways that work for you.
  As always, I encourage you to think about the ways these drug refusal skills can best be applied to your own life. In order for this material to be useful and effective, you need to make it work for you.

ADAPT: Advancing Decision Making and Problem Solving for Teens   **137**

SESSION 7

SAMPLE SESSION

4 **Guide students through the Drug Refusal Role-Play.** Start by drawing the following table on the whiteboard:

SCENARIO	PEOPLE	PLACES/SITUATIONS	DRUG
1	M, R, O	Park, O's house	Alcohol
2			
3			

The Drug Refusal Role-Play:

1. Ask a student to generate a scenario by filling in the table.

   I've drawn a table on the board. I need a volunteer to help me fill it out.

   Thanks, Megan, for volunteering. I'm going to have you help me fill out a scenario, or example. First, who are the people most likely to offer you drugs? You can just give me initials and I'll write them under "People." M, R, and O.

   OK. And what are the situations or places that you are likely to be offered drugs? The park and O's house.

   Now tell me what type of drug you are most likely to be offered by M, R, and O in those specific situations or places. Probably alcohol.

2. Have the student role-play refusing drugs using the scenario. Discuss with the group.

   Good, now tell me how you would effectively refuse drugs. You can use number 2 on your worksheet to help you. I'll pretend I'm O. Hey, I have a six-pack in my room. No, let's go watch TV with your family. I'm going to lose all privileges if I get caught drinking again.

   How did Megan do? Angie? She did great. She answered right away.
   Excellent. I also noticed she used a firm voice.
   Angie? She also came up with something else for them to do.
   Megan? It was kind of lame, but I couldn't think of anything else.
   Then we should talk about other things that would have worked . . .

3. If the student needs help, ask the group for suggestions.

4. Repeat with other students as time permits.

How Do I Refuse Drugs?

ENDING THE SESSION

1 **Have students clarify what they learned.**

Ask students what they found most helpful about drug refusal skills and how they might use the skills.

Before we end today, I want to know what you thought about the drug refusal skills we discussed. Specifically, what things do you like about them and what things may be hard to do?

2 **Pass out the Session 7 Practice Sheet, Effectively Refusing Drugs (Reproducible 7-3).**

- Walk students through the practice sheet.

  I've handed everyone a practice sheet entitled "Effectively Refusing Drugs." This sheet presents four scenarios. In each of the scenarios, imagine that you are being asked the question, "Hey, here's some marijuana. You want some?" Your task is to use the skills we learned today to effectively refuse drugs in each scenario. At the bottom of the sheet is a place for you to write in your own scenario. Use this opportunity to write in a scenario that really makes sense for you.

  Are there any questions?

- Remind students to use past examples or imagine what they would do in certain situations to complete the practice sheet.

  Just like with previous practice sheets, don't expose yourself to drugs in order to complete the practice sheet. Use past experiences or imagine what you would do in the situation.

- Remind students that their practice sheets are due at the beginning of the next session, where they will be reviewed in the group.

  Great, I look forward to reviewing these with you next week. Have a great week!

SESSION REFERENCES

Assertive Communication Skills: Monti et al., 2002; Sampl & Kadden, 2001.
Exercise: Kadden et al., 1999; Monti et al., 2002.
Practice Sheet: Monti et al., 2002; Sampl & Kadden, 2001.

Practice Sheet Icons

Remind students that the book indicates directions they need to read. The pencil indicates they have a writing assignment.

ADAPT: Advancing Decision Making and Problem Solving for Teens

HOW DO I COMMUNICATE BETTER WITH OTHERS?

Assertive Communication Skills

SESSION 8

Session Goals

- Students learn good communication skills.
- Students learn about the benefits and drawbacks of the four communication styles—Aggressive, Passive, Indirect, and Assertive.
- Students learn how to use I-messages.
- Students learn the listening skills of Listen, Clarify, and Recap.

Session Preparation

1. Quickly review the Session Outline.
2. Study the Sample Session and sample dialogue to help you anticipate how your students might respond to content.
3. On the whiteboard, write: Aggressive, Passive, Indirect, and Assertive.
4. Write the I-message model and three completed examples on the whiteboard (see p. 144), or plan to display Reproducible 8-1, I-Message Model.

Materials

- Presentation copy of I-Message Model (Reproducible 8-1). *Note*: Project on a document camera or enlarge (129% on 11" x 17" paper).
- For each student, one copy of:
    - Communication Skills (Reproducible 8-2)
    - Session 8 Practice Sheet, Communication Styles (Reproducible 8-3)
- Whiteboard and dry-erase markers
- Pencils for students to use during session

ABOUT THIS SKILL

It is important for adolescents to develop good communication skills in order to clearly get their message across. Good communication skills help adolescents in all of their interpersonal interactions.

CULTURAL CONGRUENCE

You may need to modify the assertive communication skills in this session so they are congruent with the culture(s) of the students in your particular group. See Section 2.2, Student Characteristics and Cultural Issues, on p. 16 for more information about this issue.

141

SESSION OUTLINE

BEGINNING THE SESSION

1 Welcome students.

2 **Review last session's practice sheets.** Discuss two or three student practice sheets.

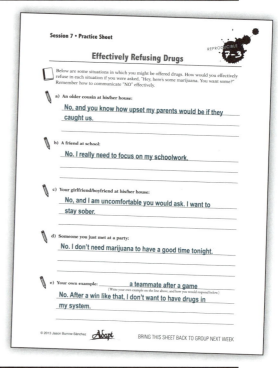

PRESENTING THE TOPIC & PRACTICING SKILLS

Communication Skills

1 **Introduce the topic of communicating effectively.** Describe the benefits of effective communication.
- Getting needs met
- Getting help from others
- Improving your relationships

2 **Introduce the four communication styles.**
- *Aggressive:* You act as if your needs are more important than anyone else's needs. Communication may be loud and in your face, and sound angry. The result may be you get what you want, but other people may avoid or not want to be with you in the future.
- *Passive:* You go along with others to avoid any argument. The result is you don't get your needs met, and you wind up angry at yourself.
- *Indirect:* You don't say what you want or need and hope other people figure out your needs. The result is you don't get your needs met and feel bad if no one figures out what is wrong.
- *Assertive:* You are direct about what you want or need. The result is you often get your needs met.

142   How Do I Communicate Better With Others?

3 **Pass out the in-session worksheet, Communication Skills (Reproducible 8-2).** Have students discuss each communication style. *Note*: You may wish to guide your discussion by writing the categories "Style," "Behavior," and "Results" on the board and making notes as students discuss the styles, as shown below.

STYLE	BEHAVIOR	RESULTS
Aggressive	Loud, angry, in your face. Bully	Get what you want, but others may avoid you
Passive	Avoid arguments. Go along with things	Avoid arguments. Feel helpless
Indirect	Don't directly say what you are thinking. Communicate with clues	Feel helpless, frustrated. Frustrates others. Feel like others don't care
Assertive	Say what you want	More likely to get what you want. Feel confident and heard

a. **Have students discuss an aggressive communication style.** Include how the person acts (looks, sounds) and the results. Then have students write a definition of the style on their worksheets.

b. **Have students discuss a passive communication style.** Include how the person acts (looks, sounds) and the results. Then have students write a definition of the style on their worksheets.

c. **Have students discuss an indirect communication style.** Include how the person acts (looks, sounds) and the results. Then have students write a definition of the style on their worksheets.

d. **Have students discuss an assertive communication style.** Include how the person acts (looks, sounds) and the results. Then have students write a definition of the style on their worksheets. Make connections to the way students practiced saying "no" to drugs in Session 7.

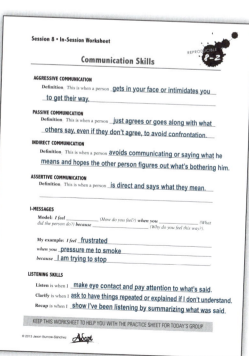

SESSION OUTLINE

4 **Teach students how to use I-messages.**

- Explain how I-messages allow you to be direct about how you feel without making other people feel they are being blamed.
- Explain the I-message model, then go through the examples with students. (*Note*: Use Reproducible 8-1 or the whiteboard model you drew before the session as a visual aid.)

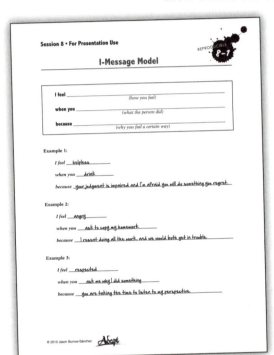

- Work through some student-generated examples of I-messages, writing their examples on the whiteboard or reproducible. Tell students I-messages are an example of assertive communication.
- Have students write an example of an I-message on their Communication Skills worksheets (Reproducible 8-2).

5 **Teach students listening skills: Listen, Clarify, and Recap.**

- Explain that good listening skills show other people that you think what they are saying is important.
- Describe each skill, then demonstrate the skill while "listening" to a student volunteer.

    a. **Listen:** Listen carefully, making no interruptions, your body facing the other person, with eye contact.
    b. **Clarify:** Ask questions if anything is unclear. Your goal is to truly understand.
    c. **Recap:** Summarize what the person has told you. Your goal is to show the person that you were listening and that you understand.

- Have students write examples of Listen, Clarify, and Recap on their worksheets.

How Do I Communicate Better With Others?

6 **Summarize.**
- Review the four communication styles, I-messages, and good listening skills.
- Encourage students to practice assertive communication, I-messages, and good listening in their daily lives.

ENDING THE SESSION

1 **Have students clarify what they learned.**
- Ask students what they found most helpful about assertive communication, I-messages, and listening skills.
- Ask them how they might use the communication skills.

2 **Pass out the Session 8 Practice Sheet, Communication Styles (Reproducible 8-3).**
- Walk students through the practice sheet.
- Remind students that their practice sheets are due at the beginning of the next group session, when they will be reviewed in the group.

Practice Sheet Icons

Remind students that the book indicates directions they need to read. The pencil indicates they have a writing assignment.

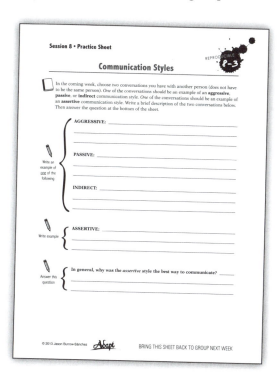

ADAPT: Advancing Decision Making and Problem Solving for Teens   145

SAMPLE SESSION

SESSION 8

BEGINNING THE SESSION

1 **Welcome students.**

2 **Review last session's practice sheets.** Discuss two or three student practice sheets.

Your task was to write down how you would respond to the question: "Hey, here's some marijuana. You want some?" Who would like to start?

I liked the examples each of you gave for refusing drugs. You've shared some great examples of how to refuse drugs effectively.

Because effective communication is so important, we are going to spend today talking more about communication.

PRESENTING THE TOPIC & PRACTICING SKILLS

Communication Skills

1 **Introduce the topic of communicating effectively.** Describe the benefits of effective communication.

- Getting needs met
- Getting help from others
- Improving your relationships

Effective communication skills are important for everyone. By communicating effectively, we can get our needs met, get the support we need from others when we're facing a challenging problem, and also improve our relationships with people we care about.

This week we are going to learn new, effective communication skills, and we'll also learn about ineffective communication styles.

Does anyone have questions? Ryan? *I think I already learned some of this stuff in another class.*

That doesn't surprise me. Some of you may already be familiar with the communication skills we are going to cover. That's OK, though. Being a good communicator takes a lot of practice.

How Do I Communicate Better With Others?

SESSION 8

2 Introduce the four communication styles.

- *Aggressive:* You act as if your needs are more important than anyone else's needs. Communication may be loud and in your face, and sound angry. The result may be you get what you want, but other people may avoid or not want to be with you in the future.
- *Passive:* You go along with others to avoid any argument. The result is you don't get your needs met, and you wind up angry at yourself.
- *Indirect:* You don't say what you want or need and hope other people figure out your needs. The result is you don't get your needs met and feel bad if no one figures out what is wrong.
- *Assertive:* You are direct about what you want or need. The result is you often get your needs met.

There are four basic communication styles: aggressive, passive, indirect, and assertive. In the last session we discussed ways to clearly communicate saying "no" to drugs. That would be an example of being assertive.

Today, we are going to work on understanding the different styles. We've all used each of the styles at one time or another.

3 Pass out the in-session worksheet, Communication Skills (Reproducible 8-2). Have students discuss each communication style. *Note*: You may wish to guide your discussion by writing the categories "Style," "Behavior," and "Results" on the board and making notes as students discuss the styles, as shown below.

a. Have students discuss an aggressive communication style. Include how the person acts (looks, sounds) and the results. Then have students write a definition of the style on their worksheets.

WHITE-BOARD

STYLE	BEHAVIOR	RESULTS
Aggressive	Loud, angry In your face Bully	Get what you want, but others may avoid you

Let's start with aggressive communication styles. When you think of someone being aggressive, what comes to mind? Maria? Well, I think of someone being mean—maybe yelling, definitely not being nice.

Yes, you are on the right track.

Someone who has an aggressive communication style uses a raised voice and possibly yells.

ADAPT: Advancing Decision Making and Problem Solving for Teens   **147**

SAMPLE SESSION

This person often seems angry or upset. Someone with an aggressive communication style looks out for his or her needs while ignoring the needs of others. Because of that, most people don't want to be around someone who uses an aggressive communication style. Let's summarize that on the board. The style is aggressive. The behavior is . . . loud, angry, in your face . . .

I'm going to write that on the board, so we know what an aggressive style sounds and looks like.

We also define an aggressive communication style as when a person acts as if what he or she wants is more important than what anyone else wants. In fact, these people typically ignore other people altogether.

Now let's think about why people might use an aggressive communication style. Here's one reason. It gets them what they want immediately. Megan? It's like being a bully.

Exactly. Now let's think about the consequences or the results. How do others respond? Angie? Well, some kids go along with it, but they don't like it.

Yes, the problem is that most of us don't like being treated aggressively. Rather than building relationships, in the long run people who communicate aggressively damage relationships with everyone around them.

Can you think of examples of when you have used an aggressive communication style, or when someone has used one with you? Ryan? Sometimes when I get into arguments with my older brother, it turns into a shouting match. He usually gets me to back down because I get tired of dealing with him.

So what do you feel like after an interaction like that with your brother? I usually feel tired and like he totally got his way. I don't like to be around him.

That sounds like aggressive communication. What about you, Angie?
That's how I act with my younger sister. I mean, if she is not listening and I really want to her to do something, I get in her face. She usually backs down. I never thought about how it makes her feel, but she's usually mad for a couple of days. That sounds like another example of aggressive communication.

Megan, Ryan, Angie—thanks for sharing those examples. We all communicate aggressively from time to time.

Here are some other examples of aggressive communication that you might have heard.

- I'm going to skip class. I don't care if you want to or not—come with me.
- I don't care if you're worried about getting in trouble—let's smoke marijuana!
- What's your problem? I want to go to the party, so let's go!
- Don't worry so much. You won't get caught, trust me.

Before we move on, write down your own definition of aggressive communication on your worksheet.

How Do I Communicate Better With Others?

SESSION 8

b. **Have students discuss a passive communication style.**
Include how the person acts (looks, sounds) and the results.
Then have students write a definition of the style on their
worksheets.

WHITE-
BOARD

STYLE	BEHAVIOR	RESULTS
Passive	Avoid confrontations Go along with things	Avoid arguments Feel helpless

The next type of communication is passive. People who communicate passively usually want to avoid any arguments. They quickly and easily go along with what other people want.

For passive communication, what is the behavior? How does the person act? Well, you said they avoid arguments. They just go along with things. What's wrong with that?

Good question. When people engage in passive communication, they also don't tell anybody what they need. Then they get angry at themselves for not getting their needs met.

In the short term, this communication style can be effective for avoiding disagreements, but in the long term these people usually feel bad about themselves for not communicating effectively with others.

Can you think of examples of when you have used a passive communication style, or someone has used one with you? Maria? Sometimes I have a hard time saying "no" to my friends when they ask me to do things that I probably shouldn't.

Can you give us an example? Yeah, when my friends want to skip fourth period. I know I shouldn't, but I do anyway. I usually just go along with it.

So, you don't tell your friends that you really don't want to skip? Right.

How do you feel afterward? Pretty lousy, especially if I get in trouble. I usually tell myself that I'm not going to go along, but I have a hard time doing that.

Angie, you are nodding your head. Yeah, that happens to me, too, with some of my friends. It's just easier to go along with what my friends want. I know it sounds stupid, but I just have a hard time sticking up for myself.

No, it doesn't sound stupid at all. It just sounds like passive communication.

We all communicate passively from time to time. Here are some examples of passive communication.

- *I'll skip class if you want to. I really don't care.*
- *Whatever you want to do is fine with me.*

ADAPT: Advancing Decision Making and Problem Solving for Teens   **149**

SAMPLE SESSION

- You decide what we do. I'm not good at making decisions.
- It's no problem—let's just do what you want.

Before we move on, write down your own definition of passive communication on your worksheets.

c. Have students discuss an indirect communication style.
Include how the person acts (looks, sounds) and the results. Then have students write a definition of the style on their worksheets.

> **WHITEBOARD**
>
> | STYLE | BEHAVIOR | RESULTS |
> |---|---|---|
> | Indirect | Don't directly say what you are thinking. Communicate with clues | Feel helpless, frustrated. Frustrates others. Feel like others don't care |

The next type of communication is indirect. People who communicate indirectly don't get to the point of what they want or need but go around it and hope that that other person figures it out.

If they are troubled, they hope other people will figure out what is bothering them. They provide clues about what they want to communicate but don't say it directly.

This type of communication style may leave people feeling bad because they don't get their needs met. People who use indirect communication may become frustrated because others don't understand what they want or need. And others may become frustrated with them.

Can you think of examples of when you have used an indirect communication style? I'm not really sure what you mean.

Have you ever been upset with someone, but instead of telling them what is bothering you, you got real quiet or avoided them? Angie? Yeah, I call it the silent treatment. I do that all the time with my boyfriend. (Group laughs)

Why? Well, because he is being a jerk.
But why is he being a jerk? Usually he's done something I don't like—like talking to another girl he knows I can't stand.

Why don't you just tell him what you think he's done wrong? I think he should figure it out on his own.

Do you think that's an effective way to communicate? No, I guess not.
Does it work? Well, he usually gets mad, then we fight, then we make up. So, yeah, in the end it usually works.

How Do I Communicate Better With Others?

But when does it work? After we have talked about it.

So, talking about what the problem actually is—in this case, your boyfriend talking to another girl—is what helped solve it?
Yeah, I guess so.

Megan, looks like you have a question. No, I mean, I get what you are saying. If Angie had just told him in the first place, they could have avoided the fighting and all the drama.
Yes, exactly. Yeah, I hate it when my friends do that to me.
What do you mean, Megan? When they all of a sudden get mad at me but don't tell me why.

How does that usually go? Similar to what Angie said. We ignore each other for a few days, then get into an argument, then realize we are fighting over something stupid, then we are friends again. I just get tired of the drama.

Yes, indirect communication often creates drama that probably doesn't need to be there. It's easier to communicate effectively in the first place.

Thanks for sharing those examples. We all communicate indirectly from time to time. Here are some examples of indirect communication.

- *Ignoring, avoiding, or not talking to someone, including what we call the silent treatment.*
- *Sending a text or e-mail that hints at the problem instead of telling someone directly what the problem is.*
- *Coming home late or showing up late to class or work because you are upset about something rather than talking to parents, a teacher, or the boss directly.*
- *Hinting at what you want instead of stating it directly. For example, you say, "It's getting late" or "Aren't you getting tired?" instead of saying you want to leave.*
- *Saying or thinking, "You should know what is bothering me."*
- *Saying or thinking, "If you really cared, you would know why I am upset."*
- *Saying or thinking, "Figure it out on your own. I shouldn't have to tell you why I'm mad."*

Before we move on, write your own definition of indirect communication on your worksheets.

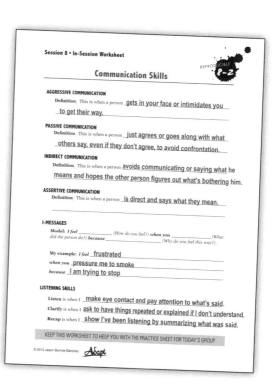

ADAPT: Advancing Decision Making and Problem Solving for Teens

SAMPLE SESSION

d. Have students discuss an assertive communication style.
Include how the person acts (looks, sounds) and the results. Then have students write a definition of the style on their worksheets. Make connections to the way students practiced saying "no" to drugs in Session 7.

> **STYLE** — Assertive
> **BEHAVIOR** — You are direct about what you want
> **RESULTS** — Often get needs met / Feel confident and heard
>
> *WHITEBOARD*

The last communication style we're going to talk about is assertive communication.

People who communicate assertively are direct about what they want from others. They clearly express their thoughts and feelings in a way that leaves little room for confusion. They can communicate confidently without being aggressive, and they are not passive or indirect. This type of communication style usually gets the person's needs met. Can you think of examples of when you have used an assertive communication style, or someone has used one with you? Jamal? Yeah, we talked about how to do this last time.

Have you communicated with anyone assertively since our last session?
Yeah. Last week, one of my friends asked me if I wanted to smoke marijuana. I told him that I didn't and not to bug me about it. I told him that I don't want to get into any more trouble. He left me alone. It worked.

So, communicating assertively got your point—to not smoke marijuana—clearly across to your friend? Yeah. Good for you, Jamal!

Thanks for sharing those examples. It is important that we all learn how to communicate assertively in order to get our needs met. Here are some examples of assertive communication:

- *I've quit smoking weed and I'd like it if you would not ask me to smoke with you anymore. I'd still like to hang out with you and do other things, but I won't do that if you keep asking me to use.*
- *I don't want to skip class. That is not the best choice for me.*
- *Please don't tell me not to worry if I get in trouble. I'm the one who has to suffer the consequences, not you.*

Before we move on write down your own definition of assertive communication on your worksheets.

There is nothing wrong with being assertive and asking for what you want as long as it's reasonable and respectful. Others will typically respond to you positively when you clearly state what you need. It is important to remember that other people also have the right to say "no," but the more clearly and assertively you state your needs, the less likely this will be.

Most of us are not born with good communication skills and therefore need to develop them just like anything else we want to improve. Do you have any questions about the communication styles we have discussed?

 Teach students how to use I-messages.

- Explain how I-messages allow you to be direct about how you feel without making other people feel they are being blamed.

  One reason that communication breaks down is because people may feel like they are being blamed for something. When people feel like they're being blamed, they focus more on arguing about why they are "right" instead of being open to hearing the other person. In fact, feeling blamed usually shuts down effective communication.

  People typically feel blamed when they hear "you" messages. Examples of "you" messages include:

  - *You don't listen to me!*
  - *You never trust me!*
  - *You are always on my case!*
  - *You don't care about me!*

  In order to increase effective communication, use I-messages. I-messages tell people how you feel about their behavior and the reason why. I-messages make people more open to listening and more likely to seriously consider what you have to say. I-messages increase effective communication.

- Explain the I-message model, then go through the examples with students. (*Note*: Use Reproducible 8-1 or the whiteboard model you drew before the session as a visual aid.)

```
I feel _____
             (how you feel)
when you _____
             (what the person did)
because _____
             (why you feel a certain way)
```

Look at the template of the I-message. You start with "I feel." Next, you say what the person did. Then you finish with how that behavior made you feel. I feel blank when you blank because blank.

Here's an example of how to use an I-message. Listen to me fill in the blanks that answer how I felt when someone did something I didn't like, and why.

ADAPT: Advancing Decision Making and Problem Solving for Teens

SAMPLE SESSION

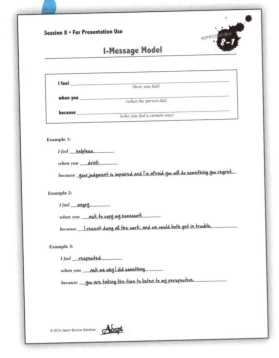

I feel <u>helpless</u> when you <u>drink</u> because <u>your judgment is impaired and I'm afraid you will do something you regret</u>.

Continue with the other I-message examples on the I-Message Model (Reproducible 8-1).

- Work through some student-generated examples of I-messages, writing their examples on the whiteboard or reproducible. Tell students I-messages are an example of assertive communication.

Will, do you want to help with me with an example? Please fill in the blanks. I feel <u>mad</u> when you <u>don't listen to me</u> because <u>I think you don't care what I think</u>.

Good example. Who might you say this to? Probably my mom. She doesn't always listen to me, but I've never really thought about why it makes me mad.

Can you try using an I-message with your mom? Sure. We usually end up in an argument and I just leave. *So, if this prevents an argument with your mom, it's worth trying?* Maybe.

OK, Angie, help me with another example. I feel <u>angry</u> when you <u>immediately blame me for something</u> because <u>I can't tell you my side of the story</u>." Another good example. Who are you saying this to? Probably my parents because, like Will said, they don't listen to me. *Do you think you could try this with your parents?* I could give it a try. It's better than arguing with them because that never gets me anywhere.

OK, a couple more examples. Ryan? I feel <u>upset</u> when you <u>offer me marijuana</u> because <u>I'm trying to stop using it</u>. Who are you saying this to? One of my friends.

Good. Megan? I feel <u>annoyed</u> when you <u>keep asking me to skip school</u> because <u>I need to improve my attendance</u>. Who are you saying this to? A friend who always wants me to skip with him.

Sounds like you have this! You can see from the board that I-messages consist of telling someone how you feel about their behavior and then the reason you feel this way. Let's look at the examples on the board. In the first example, Will is saying he is mad because his mother didn't listen to him and it makes him feel like his mother doesn't care about what he thinks.

In the second example, Angie is saying that she feels angry because her parents are quick to blame her before hearing her side of the situation.

I-messages are usually less likely to make someone else feel like you are blaming them. Instead, you are simply telling how you feel about something the person did and giving a reason why.

How Do I Communicate Better With Others?

This is another form of assertive communication. You are clearly stating how you feel about something, and there is nothing wrong with that. One of the keys to using I-messages is to focus on what the person actually did (behavior) because he or she can change behavior.

Communication is more likely to break down when you focus on the person. For example, by saying, "You are bad at listening to me" or "You are such a loser for asking me to do that." In those examples, the person is more likely to feel like you are attacking them personally instead of asking them to change a behavior. Do you have any questions about using I-messages?

- Have students write an example of an I-message on their Communication Skills worksheets.

  Before we move on, write your own example of an I-message on your worksheet.

 Teach students listening skills: Listen, Clarify, and Recap.

- Explain that good listening skills show other people that you think what they are saying is important.

  The other communication skill that I want to talk about is how to listen to another person. Listening is a really important part of effective communication, and it takes some practice to get good at it.

  Being a good listener shows other people that you think what they're saying is important. Think about the times when you felt someone wasn't listening to you and how that made you feel. Who has some examples of times when you were not listened to? Will? Well, like I said before, sometimes my mom doesn't listen to me.

  How does that make you feel? Like she really doesn't think what I am saying is important.

  What about you? Have there been times when you weren't listening to someone? Yeah, probably with my mom. Sometimes I just tune her out or leave.

  How do you think that makes her feel? Probably like what she is saying is not important because I don't want to hear it.

  Yes, that would be my guess. All of us are guilty of not being good listeners from time to time, but there are some things you can do to improve your listening skills. Listening skills are not hard, but they do require practice.

- Describe each skill, then demonstrate the skill while "listening" to a student volunteer.

  We are going to discuss three listening skills that will help you communicate effectively with others. Look at the bottom of your worksheet.

  The three skills are Listen, Clarify, and Recap. Let's go through each one and talk about what it means.

ADAPT: Advancing Decision Making and Problem Solving for Teens

SESSION 8

SAMPLE SESSION

a. **Listen:** Listen carefully, making no interruptions, your body facing the other person, with eye contact.

The first skill is Listen. When you listen, you pay careful attention to what the other person is saying. Position your body facing him or her and make eye contact. Don't say anything to interrupt and use your body language, such as nodding your head, to show that you are listening. Your goal is to make sure the other person knows that you are listening to him or her.

Sometimes it's easier to understand something by seeing the opposite of how it's supposed to look. I'm going to show you poor listening skills first. Megan, will you help me with this? Sure.

Megan, spend a couple of minutes telling me about your day yesterday and what you did. OK, yesterday I . . .

While the student is talking, do not make direct eye contact or face the student, and look generally bored by what the student is saying.

Thanks, Megan. Now I want you to tell me about your day again, and I will respond with good listening skills. OK, yesterday I . . .

While the student is talking, make eye contact, directly face the student, and act interested in what is being said.

Thanks again, Megan. What did you notice about the first example? Well, it really seemed like you weren't interested in what I was saying. It made me feel like not talking to you anymore.

What about the second example? Well, I felt better because you were looking at me and seemed interested in what I had to say. It made me feel like what I was saying was important to you. It made me want to talk more.

b. **Clarify:** Ask questions if anything is unclear. Your goal is to truly understand.

If something is unclear, ask the person to repeat what he or she said or ask specific questions for clarification. Your goal is to make sure you understand what the other person said.

Jamal, will you help me demonstrate this skill? Sure.

Jamal, spend a couple of minutes telling me about your day yesterday and what you did. OK, yesterday I . . .

While the student is talking, listen to what the student is saying and, at appropriate points, ask for clarification. You might say things such as, "I want to make sure I understand what you are saying, so tell me again what that person said" or "I'm not clear on that—how did it happen again?"

Provide additional examples of clarifying as needed to demonstrate this skill.

156   How Do I Communicate Better With Others?

c. **Recap:** Summarize what the person has told you. Your goal is to show the person you were listening and you understand.

After the person is done speaking, briefly summarize what the person said to you. This shows that you were listening and allows the person to correct anything that you may have misunderstood. Your goal is to show the other person you were listening and to make sure you understand his or her message.

Jamal, will you continue helping me in demonstrating this last skill? Sure.

Jamal, you just told me about your day yesterday, and I want to make sure I understand you correctly. It sounds like overall your day was good—you went to school as usual and generally liked the material in all of your classes. After school, you went to the park and skateboarded with some friends. Does that sound right? Well, actually, I had to go home first and do my homework because my mom wants me to finish it before I do anything else after school.

Yes, you did mention that. Thanks for correcting me. You went home first and did your homework before going to the park to skateboard. Does that sound more accurate? Yeah, it does. Did I miss anything? No, not really—it sounds right.

Provide additional examples of recapping as needed to demonstrate this skill.

- Have students write examples of Listen, Clarify, and Recap on their worksheets.

Before we move on, write down your own examples of these three listening skills on your worksheets.

9 Summarize.

- Review the four communication styles, I-messages, and good listening skills.

As we discussed, it is important to be an effective communicator in order to get your needs met. There are four basic communication styles: aggressive, passive, indirect, and assertive. In general, an assertive communication style works best. You can also increase your ability to communicate effectively by using I-messages and practicing good listening skills.

- Encourage students to practice assertive communication, I-messages, and good listening skills in their daily lives.

I encourage you to practice the skills we learned today in your daily lives. These skills can help in a number of areas and improve your relationships with others. It is important that you make these skills work for you, and you need to practice them in order to do that.

ADAPT: Advancing Decision Making and Problem Solving for Teens   **157**

SESSION 8

SAMPLE SESSION

ENDING THE SESSION

1 **Have students clarify what they learned.**
- Ask students what they found most helpful about assertive communication, I-messages, and listening skills.
- Ask them how they might use the communication skills.

    Before we end today, I want to know what you thought about the communication skills we discussed. Specifically, what things do you like about them and what things may be hard to do?

2 **Pass out the Session 8 Practice Sheet, Communication Styles (Reproducible 8-3).**
- Walk students through the practice sheet.

    I've handed everyone a practice sheet called Communication Styles. This sheet requires you to choose two conversations that you have in the coming week. One of the conversations should be an example of an aggressive, passive, or indirect style. Write that example down on the top part of the sheet.

    The second conversation should be an example of Assertive Communication. Write that example in the middle of the sheet.

    These conversations do not need to be with the same person. At the bottom of the sheet, use your examples to explain why assertive is typically the best communication style. You can use the worksheets you completed today to help you with the practice sheet.

- Remind students that their practice sheets are due at the beginning of the next group session, when they will be reviewed in the group.

> **Practice Sheet Icons**
>
> Remind students that the book indicates directions they need to read. The pencil indicates they have a writing assignment.

SESSION REFERENCES
Communication Styles: Monti et al., 2002; Webb et al., 2002.
I-messages: Burr, 1990; Erford et al., 2010.
Listening Skills: Monti et al., 2002; Webb et al., 2002.
Practice Sheet: Monti et al., 2002.

How Do I Communicate Better With Others?

HOW DO I MANAGE MY ANGER?

Session Goals

- Students learn that it is normal to experience anger from time to time.
- Students learn that managing anger involves recognizing their body cues, thoughts, and feelings in response to external triggers.
- Students learn how manage anger by Recognizing their anger, Reviewing options, and Responding effectively (R^3).
- Students learn that a calm response to anger can pave the way for effective problem solving.

ABOUT THIS SKILL

Everybody experiences angry emotions at times, but many students do not have effective ways to manage their anger. Learning skills to manage anger will help students deal more effectively with situations that trigger their anger.

Session Preparation

1. Quickly review the Session Outline.
2. Study the Sample Session and sample dialogue to help you anticipate how your students might respond to content. *Note*: Carefully study the R-Cubed (R^3) Method for effectively managing anger.
3. Display Reproducible 9-1 or draw a template of the R^3 Model on the whiteboard (see p. 161 for example).

Materials

- Presentation copy of Managing Anger: R-Cubed (R^3) Model (Reproducible 9-1). *Note*: Project on a document camera or enlarge (129% on 11" x 17" paper).
- For each student, one copy of:
  - R-Cubed (R^3) Model to Manage (Reproducible 9-2)
  - Session 9 Practice Sheet, Anger Management Using the R-Cubed (R^3) Model (Reproducible 9-3)
- Whiteboard and dry-erase markers
- Pencils for students to use during session

SESSION OUTLINE

BEGINNING THE SESSION

1 Welcome students.

2 **Review last session's practice sheets.** Discuss two or three student practice sheets. Ask students what they learned about communication styles from the assignment.

Practice Sheet Completion

- Acknowledge successes—completed practice sheets.
- Address challenges—lost or incomplete practice sheets.
- Summarize steps to successful completion.

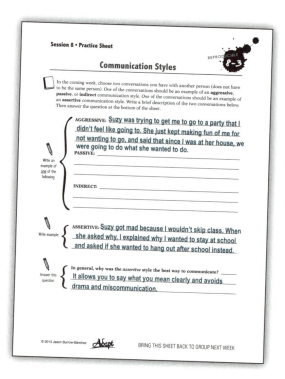

PRESENTING THE TOPIC & PRACTICING SKILLS

Anger Management Skills

1 **Introduce the topic of anger management.** Explain that effectively managing your anger always leads to better outcomes.

- Ask students if they have learned anger management skills in other classes. If students already understand anger management, spend more time on skill practice.
- Have students share examples of times when they were angry and things did not turn out well.
- Have students share examples of people in their lives who do not manage anger well and people who do manage anger well.
- Discuss how decision-making and problem-solving skills are diminished when we are angry.

160   How Do I Manage My Anger?

2 **Review anger triggers.** Pass out the R-Cubed (R³) Model to Manage Anger worksheets (Reproducible 9-2) to students.

- Direct students' attention to the words "Anger Triggers" on the whiteboard or your display of Reproducible 9-1. Remind students about the role of triggers in mapping problem behaviors (Sessions 4 and 5).
- List student-generated examples of anger triggers.
- Have students write their personal anger triggers on their worksheets.

3 **Introduce the R-Cubed (R³) Model for effectively managing anger.**

a. **Discuss the first R.** Recognize you are angry.

- Have students answer the question, "How do I recognize I am angry?" by discussing body cues. Write responses on the board.
- Have students write examples of body cues on their worksheets.
- Have students answer the question, "How do I recognize I am angry?" by discussing angry thoughts. Write student responses on the board.
- Have students write examples of angry thoughts on their worksheets.
- Have students answer the question, "How do I recognize I am angry?" by discussing feelings. Write responses on the board.
- Have students write examples of angry feelings on their worksheets.
- Explain that being aware of body cues, thoughts, and feelings can help students recognize when they are angry.

b. **Discuss the second R.** Review your options.

- Have students answer the question, "What can I do to calm down and help me successfully manage my anger?" Write their responses on the board.
- Have students write their options for calming down on their worksheets.

c. **Discuss the third R.** Respond effectively.

- Have students tell you their top two options for calming down. Write student responses on the board. Then have students write their top two choices on their worksheets.
- Have students discuss problem solving.

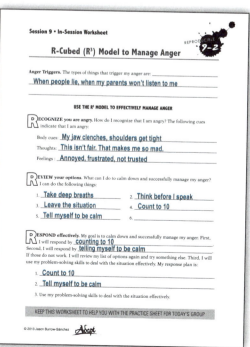

ADAPT: Advancing Decision Making and Problem Solving for Teens

SESSION OUTLINE

4. Summarize.
- Review the R-Cubed (R^3) Model for effectively managing anger.
- Tell students to practice anger management skills in their daily lives.

5. As time permits, guide students through anger management role-plays using their examples.
- Ask students to describe recent situations that made them angry. Write their examples on the board.
- Ask for two student volunteers to role-play an example scenario. Have one student play the angry person, while the other student plays the person who caused the situation. (*Note*: The angry person should practice the R-Cubed anger management skills. The other person should not "give in" and make the situation OK.)
- Review the role-play and what anger management skills were demonstrated well and what could be improved upon.
- Repeat the role-play with other pairs of students and other student examples.

ENDING THE SESSION

1. Have students clarify what they learned.

Ask students what they found most helpful about the R-Cubed anger management skills they learned and how they might use them.

2. Pass out the Session 9 Practice Sheet, Anger Management Using the R-Cubed (R^3) Model (Reproducible 9-3).
- Walk students through the practice sheet.
- Remind students that their practice sheets are due at the beginning of the next session, where they will be reviewed in the group.

Practice Sheet Icons

Remind students that the book indicates directions they need to read. The pencil indicates they have a writing assignment.

---

162   How Do I Manage My Anger?

SAMPLE SESSION

SESSION **9**

BEGINNING THE SESSION

1 **Welcome students.**

2 **Review last session's practice sheets.**
Discuss two or three student practice sheets. Ask students what they learned about communication styles from the assignment.

Your task was to write down one example of aggressive, passive, or indirect communication you experienced last week, then write down one example of assertive communication. Who would like to start?

Remember that in most situations an assertive style is effective. Continue to practice the communication skills we learned in your daily lives.

Session 8 • Practice Sheet

REPRODUCIBLE **8-3**

Communication Styles

In the coming week, choose *two* conversations you have with another person (does not have to be the same person). *One* of the conversations should be an example of an **aggressive**, **passive**, or **indirect** communication style. *One* of the conversations should be an example of an **assertive** communication style. Write a brief description of the two conversations below. Then answer the question at the bottom of the sheet.

Write an example of *one* of the following

AGGRESSIVE: Suzy was trying to get me to go to a party that I didn't feel like going to. She just kept making fun of me for not wanting to go, and said that since I was at her house, we were going to do what she wanted to do.

PASSIVE: _____

INDIRECT: _____

Write example

ASSERTIVE: Suzy got mad because I wouldn't skip class. When she asked why, I explained why I wanted to stay at school and asked if she wanted to hang out after school instead.

Answer this question

In general, why was the *assertive* style the best way to communicate? It allows you to say what you mean clearly and avoids drama and miscommunication.

© 2013 Jason Burrow-Sánchez — *Adapt* — BRING THIS SHEET

PRESENTING THE TOPIC & PRACTICING SKILLS

Anger Management Skills

1 **Introduce the topic of anger management.** Explain that effectively managing your anger always leads to better outcomes.
Today we are going to discuss anger. Raise your hand if you have experienced anger.

From the show of hands, it looks like everyone has been angry at one time or another. So the first thing we know about anger is that everybody experiences it. Today we are going to discuss ways to effectively manage anger.

Getting angry is normal, but anger can create problems if we don't know how to deal with it effectively. Effectively managing anger always leads to better outcomes.

- Ask students if they have learned anger management skills in other classes. If students already understand anger management, spend more time on skill practice.

> **Practice Sheet Completion**
>
> - Acknowledge successes—completed practice sheets.
> - Address challenges—lost or incomplete practice sheets.
> - Summarize steps to successful completion.

ADAPT: Advancing Decision Making and Problem Solving for Teens

163

SESSION 9

SAMPLE SESSION

- Have students share examples of times when they were angry and things did not turn out well.

  Think about the last time you were angry and it didn't turn out well. Who would like to share an example like that? Jamal? Yeah, it was this last week.

  What happened? I got into an argument with my parents. I came home late, but they weren't listening to the reason why. They just kept telling me that I was wrong and didn't hear what I had to say.

  What happened? We all ended up yelling. I got sent to my room and now I have an earlier curfew.

  Sounds like it didn't turn out well and created more problems for you. Yeah.

  That's a great example. Who has another example of getting angry?

  Will? I guess so. I've gotten into trouble for fighting.

  How does this happen? Usually some other kid says something to me that I don't like. I get angry and then we get into a fight.

  Do you think fighting is the best way to deal with someone who says something we don't like? (shrugs)

  It's important to remember that you always have other options. What were the consequences of fighting? I got suspended. My dad was mad. I almost got arrested.

  So it also created other problems? Yeah, I guess it did.

  Thanks for sharing those examples. Today we are going to discuss how you can manage anger instead of letting anger manage you.

- Have students share examples of people in their lives who do not manage anger well and people who do manage anger well.

  One reason people don't manage anger effectively is because they may not have good models. Think of an older person who influences your life. This could be a parent, an older sibling, or friend. Is that person good at managing anger? If yes, you can learn to manage your anger by watching and listening.

  Ryan, do you know someone who manages their anger well? Yeah, my mom does.

  How does she do that? Well, she usually doesn't yell or jump all over me when a problem comes up. She usually asks me about what happened first.

164   How Do I Manage My Anger?

SESSION 9

Give us a specific example. I got suspended from school last month and my mom had to come pick me up. She could have been really mad at me and yelled, and I wouldn't have blamed her for that, but instead she asked me what happened. She wanted to hear my side of the story. Then we talked about the consequences of being suspended. I ended up getting grounded, but at least I didn't get into an argument with my mom.

If you aren't around people who are good at managing anger, it is hard to learn how to do it.

Think about the people in your lives who don't handle their anger very well. Would you like to share an example? Maria? Well, I don't think my dad controls his anger very well. He always yells at us. We get tired of that.

So you don't think yelling is very effective? No, we just try to avoid him. You avoid him when he's mad, so that probably doesn't help solve the problem. No, it doesn't.

If important people in your life don't deal with anger well, that doesn't mean you can use it for an excuse. Saying "Well, my parents never taught me how to deal with my anger, so I can act any way I want" is considered a cop-out. This goes to the consequences we talked about earlier. In the end, you have to deal with consequences.

- Discuss how decision-making and problem-solving skills are diminished when we are angry.

  It is harder to make good decisions and find solutions to problems when we are angry. In fact, we know from research that the decision-making parts of our brain don't work as well when we are angry. Our ability to see all of our options becomes limited.

  If we are quick to react when angry, we are not likely to choose the best way to handle the situation. For example, have you ever heard the term "blind with rage"? It refers to being blind to other—usually more effective—options for dealing with a situation that makes us angry.

  Most of us don't like feeling angry. It's not a pleasant experience and uses up a lot of energy. Unfortunately, the things people do when angry, like yelling, fighting, and using drugs, typically create more problems.

ADAPT: Advancing Decision Making and Problem Solving for Teens **165**

SESSION 9

SAMPLE SESSION

2 **Review anger triggers.** Pass out the R-Cubed (R³) Model to Manage Anger worksheets (Reproducible 9-2) to students.

- Direct students' attention to the words "Anger Triggers" on the whiteboard or your display of Reproducible 9-1. Remind students about the role of triggers in mapping problem behaviors (Sessions 4 and 5).

    Before we discuss specific skills for effectively dealing with anger, we need to talk about anger triggers. We learned about triggers when we talked about mapping problem behaviors and alternative behaviors.

    Anger triggers are events that cause us to become angry. Examples include being blamed for something you didn't do, being yelled at by another person, having someone lie about you, and being reprimanded by a teacher in front of other students.

    Each of us has triggers for anger. A trigger for one person may not necessarily be a trigger for another person.

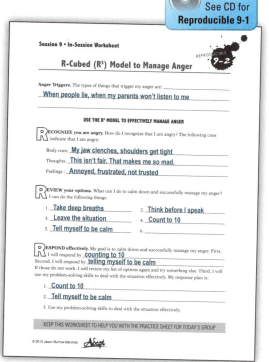

See CD for Reproducible 9-1

- List student-generated examples of anger triggers.

    I want to list some of your anger triggers. What kind of anger triggers do you have? Ryan? I don't like rude comments or when someone calls me a name or something. It makes me mad.

    Megan, what about you? I get mad when my parents don't listen to me.

    OK. What about you, Jamal? I get really mad when my friends borrow my stuff and don't return it.

WHITEBOARD

Anger Triggers

Rude comments, name calling, parents don't listen, friends borrow stuff and don't return it

---

Thank you for those examples. You can use your knowledge of anger triggers to help you understand when you are most likely to be angry. Knowing what makes

166   How Do I Manage My Anger?

you angry will help you determine when you need to use the anger management skills. Any questions about how anger triggers work?

- Have students write their personal anger triggers on their worksheets.

3. Introduce the R-Cubed (R³) Model for effectively managing anger.

To manage your anger, we are going to look at three steps—the three Rs—that we call the R-Cubed Model for managing anger. The first R is to Recognize you are angry. The second R is to Review your options, and the third R is to Respond effectively.

a. Discuss the first R. Recognize you are angry.

- Have students answer the question, "How do I recognize I am angry?" by discussing body cues. Write responses on the board.

    We all know what it feels like to be angry. Unfortunately, we usually recognize that we are angry too late, after we have already done something that created more problems, like yelling, screaming, hitting someone, or using drugs. If we can recognize that we are angry while it is happening, we can prevent more problems from occurring.

    In order to recognize anger, we need to be aware of how our body feels. Think about the last time you were angry. Try to remember what your body felt like. For some people, their shoulders tighten up, their stomach feels upset, and they feel shaky. We call these experiences body cues. Body cues are ways that our body tells us that we are angry.

    Give me some examples of what your body feels like when you are angry, and I will write them on the board.

    Maria? My stomach usually feels upset.
    Jamal? My mom says my face gets red.
    Will? I clench my fists.

> **RECOGNIZE**
> Body Cues: stomach upset, face gets red, clenched fists

- Have students write examples of body cues on their worksheets.

    We all have similarities and differences in the way our bodies feel when we are angry. On your worksheet, write down the types of body cues you have when you are angry.

SESSION 9

SAMPLE SESSION

- Have students answer the question, "How do I recognize I am angry?" by discussing their angry thoughts. Write student responses on the board.

You can also recognize that you're getting angry by being aware of what you are thinking about when you are angry. Certain types of thoughts may pop into your head after you experience anger triggers.

For example, if your mom blames you for something you didn't do, you may be thinking, "I hate it when she does this—it makes me so mad," "She never listens to my side of the story," or "People always blame me for things. I can't catch a break."

Generally, these thoughts serve only to make you angrier because you start focusing on them. What are some thoughts you have when you are angry? I'll write them on the board. It may be easier to come up with examples if you think about the last trigger or event that made you angry. I will write your examples on the board.

Ryan? I am usually thinking how unfair it is when my dad doesn't listen to me.
Angie? Sometimes I think about how I can get back at someone for saying something that I didn't like.
Maria? I usually think I'm never talking to that person again.

> WHITE-BOARD
>
> <u>RECOGNIZE</u>
>
> Body Cues: stomach upset, face gets red, clenched fists
> Thoughts: unfair, how I can get back at someone, won't talk to
>   them again

- Have students write examples of angry thoughts on their worksheets.

We all have similarities and differences in the types of thoughts we have when we are angry. On your worksheet, write down the types of thoughts you have when you are angry.

- Have students answer the question, "How do I recognize I am angry?" by discussing feelings. Write responses on the board.

Finally, we can recognize anger by being aware of what we are feeling when we are angry. After an anger trigger, you may experience certain feelings. For example, if your mom has blamed you for something, you may feel really frustrated, upset, or discouraged. If you continue to feel this way, it will only fuel your anger.

What feelings do you have when you are angry? Think about the last trigger or event that made you angry. I will write your examples on the board.

168   *How Do I Manage My Anger?*

Jamal? I feel really pissed and frustrated.
Megan? I usually feel upset and want to yell at someone.

WHITE-
BOARD

RECOGNIZE

Body Cues: stomach upset, face gets red, clenched fists
Thoughts: unfair, how I can get back at someone. won't talk to
        them again
Feelings: pissed, frustrated, upset, want to yell

- Have students write examples of angry feelings on their worksheets.

  Just like body cues and thoughts, we all have similarities and differences in the types of feelings we have when angry. On your worksheet I want you to write down the types of feelings you have when angry.

- Explain that being aware of body cues, thoughts, and feelings can help students recognize when they are angry.

  Being aware of body cues, thoughts, and feelings will help you know when you are angry or when you are starting to become angry. Some cues may be more noticeable than others, such as your shoulders tensing up versus thinking "I'm really angry she said that." Keep in mind that any of these things can help you identify when you are angry.

  Being aware of your anger is one of the first steps to managing it. After you realize that you're angry or becoming angry, you can decide what to do about it.

b. **Discuss the second R.** Review your options.

- Have students answer the question, "What can I do to calm down and help me successfully manage my anger?" Write their responses on the board.

  When you are angry, you have options for what you can do. If you focus on your anger, your options will feel limited. Ask yourself the question, "What can I do that will help me calm down and manage my anger?"

  Here are some examples. Some people count to 10 before responding when they are angry. Others take four or five deep breaths when they are angry.

  Other people talk to themselves. They say things like:

  - *I don't need to get so upset over this. It isn't a big deal.*
  - *Everything is OK. I can handle this situation.*
  - *I am upset, but I can deal with this without yelling or screaming.*
  - *I'm not going to let this person make me angry. It isn't worth it.*

ADAPT: Advancing Decision Making and Problem Solving for Teens   **169**

SESSION 9

SAMPLE SESSION

If you have a list of things that help you calm down, you can learn to successfully manage your anger.

What are examples of things you can do to calm down and manage your anger? I will write your examples on the board.

Ryan? I guess I could just walk away from the situation before I do anything.
Megan? I could take a few deep breaths.
Angie? I could tell myself that getting mad over something stupid is not worth it.

WHITEBOARD

REVIEW
- Walk away from the situation
- Take a few deep breaths
- Tell myself it's not worth getting mad over

- Have students write their options for calming down on their worksheets.

  Great examples! Thanks for sharing. On your worksheet I want you to write down your options for calming down when you are angry.

  Now each of you has a list of options you can choose from to help you calm down and manage your anger. So, if you feel angry, you can review your options.

  Your next task is to determine which of these options to use.

c. Discuss the third R. Respond effectively.

- Have students tell you their top two options for calming down. Write student responses on the board. Then have students write their top two choices on their worksheets.

  I want you to pick the top two things from your list of options that are most likely to help you calm down and manage your anger. Those two things will help you respond effectively. What are the top two options you have chosen? I will write your examples on the board.

  Will? I could probably take a few deep breaths, or count to 10 in my head.
  Angie? I could remind myself to stay calm. And tell myself it's something stupid to get mad about.
  Ryan? I could give myself a timeout (Group laughs) and walk away from another kid who makes me mad and tell myself it's not worth it.
  Megan?

How Do I Manage My Anger?

I appreciate your sharing those examples.

On your worksheets, I want you to write down the top two things you have chosen. You can do those two things to help you calm down and manage your response the next time you are angry.

- Have students discuss problem solving.

  Once you've calmed down by recognizing you're angry, reviewing your options, and responding effectively, you can use your problem-solving skills to effectively deal with the situation.

  What are some things you could do to problem solve?

  Jamal? I guess I could figure out an alternative to punching someone.
  Maria? I could use an I-message.
  Megan? I could use the 4-Ws to solve problems.

  It is much easier to problem solve and make good decisions when you are calm. Each situation that makes you angry will be different, so you can use your problem-solving skills and adapt them to the situation. Do you have any questions about responding effectively to anger and then problem solving?

4 Summarize.

- Review the R-Cubed (R^3) Model for effectively managing anger.

  As we discussed, it is important to effectively manage your anger. You want to be in control of it rather than it being in control of you.

  We discussed your anger triggers. Then we discussed the R-Cubed Model for effectively managing your anger. The first step is to Recognize that you are angry. The second step is to Review your options for dealing with your anger, and the last step is to Respond to the situation in an effective manner.

- Tell students to practice anger management skills in their daily lives.

  I encourage you to practice the skills we learned today in your daily lives. These skills can help you effectively manage your anger in many situations. You can also be a good model for others by showing them how you effectively manage your anger. It is important that you make these skills work for you and you need to practice them in order to do that.

5 As time permits, guide students through anger management role-plays using their examples.

- Ask students to describe recent situations that made them angry. Write their examples on the board.

  I want each of you to think about a recent situation that made you angry. Examples could include someone breaking something valuable to you, such as your iPod, your parents not listening to you, an argument with someone else, or

SAMPLE SESSION

something similar. I am going to write your examples on the board. Who would like to start?

Write student examples on board. Try to obtain one example from each student.

- Ask for two student volunteers to role-play an example scenario. Have one student play the angry person, while the other student plays the person who caused the situation. (*Note*: The angry person should practice the R-Cubed anger management skills. The other person should not "give in" and make the situation OK.)

  I need two volunteers to demonstrate the anger management skills we learned today using one of the examples on the board. One person will play the role of the person who is angry. The second person will play the role of the person who caused the situation. Then, if there's time, we'll reverse roles.

  Ryan. Thanks. Please pick one of the examples from the board.
  OK. Let's do the one where the mom is yelling at me because I was out late.

  Who would like to play the role of the mom? Angie. Great.

  Angie: Ryan, I am really mad at you. You were supposed to be home two hours ago.
  Ryan: Let me explain.
  Angie: I don't want to hear a word from you. You are late—no excuses!
  Ryan: One, two, three, four . . .

- Review the role-play and what anger management skills were demonstrated well and what could be improved on.

  Thanks to Ryan and Angie for participating in that exercise. I want to spend a few minutes discussing the situation and what anger management skills were demonstrated. Angie, great job. You sounded like a very upset mom. Ryan, you did a nice job using a response that would calm you down.

  Angie, if you really were Ryan's mom, how would you have responded?
  I would have told him to quit being a smart aleck.

  Ryan, what could you have done to calm down without making the situation worse? I should have counted in my head.

  Good. And then you could have used an I-message. Ryan, what would that have sounded like? Mom, I feel upset when you don't let me explain because it makes me feel like I don't have a chance to tell you about the problem I had.

  Have students reverse roles, then conduct another brief discussion, as time allows.

- Repeat the role-play with other pairs of students and other student examples.

172 How Do I Manage My Anger?

ENDING THE SESSION

1 **Have students clarify what they learned.**

Ask students what they found most helpful about the anger management skills they learned and how they might use them.

Before we end today, I want to know what you thought about the anger management skills we discussed. Specifically, what things do you like about them and what things may be hard to do?

2 **Pass out the Session 9 Practice Sheet, Anger Management Using the R-Cubed (R³) Model (Reproducible 9-3).**

- Walk students through the practice sheet.

  I've handed everyone a practice sheet called Anger Management Using the R-Cubed Model. This assignment requires you to choose one situation in the coming week that makes you angry. First, you need to describe the situation and include any specific triggers that caused the anger. Second, you need to describe how you used the R-Cubed Model to effectively deal with the situation. This includes describing how you recognized you were angry. Make sure to mention specific body cues, thoughts, and feelings.

  You will then need to list the specific options you reviewed for effectively managing the situation. Finally, you will need to describe how you responded to the situation. You can use the in-session worksheet you completed today to help you with the practice sheet.

  Remember, the picture of the book indicates the directions you need to read for completing the sheet. The picture of the pencil indicates you have a writing assignment. Are there any questions?

- Remind students that their practice sheets are due at the beginning of the next session, where they will be reviewed in the group.

  Great, I look forward to reviewing these with you next week. Have a great week!

Practice Sheet Icons

Remind students that the book indicates directions they need to read. The pencil indicates they have a writing assignment.

SESSION REFERENCES

R-Cubed Model: Monti et al., 2002; Reilly & Shopshire, 2002; Webb et al., 2002.
Practice Sheet: Monti et al., 2002; Webb et al., 2002.

ADAPT: Advancing Decision Making and Problem Solving for Teens   173

HOW DO I MANAGE MY NEGATIVE MOOD?

SESSION 10

Session Goals

- Students learn that negative moods are normal from time to time.
- Students learn that managing negative moods involves recognizing their internal reactions—thoughts and feelings—to external situations.
- Students learn effective mood management skills.

Session Preparation

1. Quickly review the Session Outline.
2. Study the Sample Session and sample dialogue to help you anticipate how your students might respond to content.
3. Before the session starts, draw the Negative Mood Model (see Figure 10-1 on p. 177) on the whiteboard. Also draw a blank Mood Model. Or plan to display Reproducible 10-1, Mood Model.
4. Before the session, study Martin and Sam's Parent Criticism Scenarios on pp. 183–185.

Materials

- Presentation copy of Mood Model (Reproducible 10-1)
  Note: Project on a document camera or enlarge (129% on 11" x 17" paper).
- For each student, one copy of:
  - Negative Thoughts Chart (Reproducible 10-1)
  - Activities I Enjoy (Reproducible 10-2)
  - Session 10 Practice Sheet, Managing Negative Moods Using the R-Cubed (R^3) Model (Reproducible 10-3)
- Whiteboard and dry-erase markers
- Pencils for students to use during session

ABOUT THIS SKILL

A brief negative mood is normal. Managing a negative mood prevents it from becoming worse.

DISCLAIMER

This session is not intended as a treatment for major depression. If you suspect a student is experiencing a major depressive episode or dysthymia, referral for appropriate assessment is warranted. In addition, if a student makes any mention of hurting him/herself, immediate referral to a professional is warranted after making sure the student is not in any immediate danger. If you are in doubt, consult immediately with a professional. Prior to this session, find out where you can send a student for professional help. Also be familiar with any state, district, and school policies regarding students who appear depressed or threaten suicide.

SESSION OUTLINE

BEGINNING THE SESSION

1 Welcome students.

2 **Review last session's practice sheets.** Discuss two or three student practice sheets.

- Ask students what they learned about anger management from the assignment.
- Thank students and encourage them to continue to use the anger management skills in their daily life.

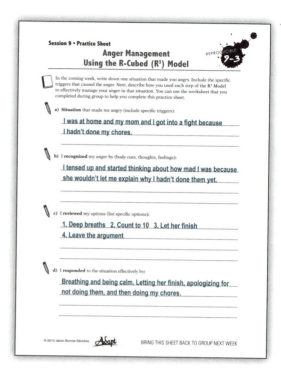

PRESENTING THE TOPIC & PRACTICING SKILLS

Mood Management Skills

1 **Introduce the topic of mood management.** Explain that brief negative moods are normal.

- Ask students how they describe negative or depressive moods.
- Explain that negative moods that get worse or last a long time are problems.
- Explain that negative moods can lead to bad decisions.
- Explain that negative moods can be managed.

176   *How Do I Manage My Negative Mood?*

2 **Direct students to the Mood Model on the board (or the display of Reproducible 10-1).** Explain that the model will help them understand why people experience negative moods.

Figure 10-1
Mood Model

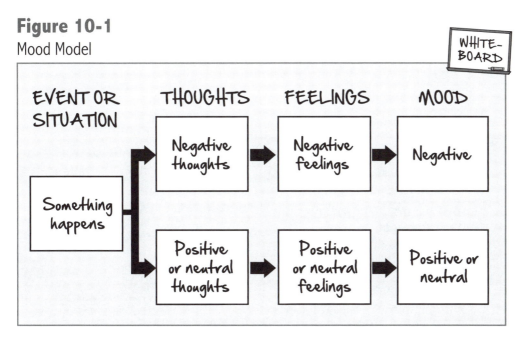

- Work through Martin's Parent Criticism Scenario, filling in the top row of the blank Mood Model as you go (see Figure 10-2 below for Martin and Sam's completed scenarios).

Figure 10-2
Martin and Sam's Parent Criticism Scenario

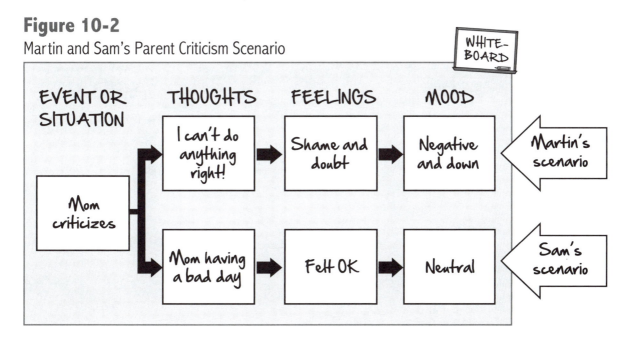

ADAPT: Advancing Decision Making and Problem Solving for Teens

SESSION 10

SESSION OUTLINE

- Emphasize the need for students to stop and think about negative thoughts because they occur so quickly.
- Work through and compare Sam's Parent Criticism Scenario, filling in the bottom row of the blank Mood Model as you go. As you work through Sam's scenario, discuss how his reactions are different than Martin's, even though the trigger is the same. Emphasize that it is Martin's negative thoughts and not the event itself that led to his negative mood.

3 **Hand out the Negative Thoughts Chart (Reproducible 10-2).** Tell the students they will learn about different kinds of negative thoughts that can lead to negative moods and also how to challenge those negative thoughts. Explain that having negative thoughts from time to time is normal, but it becomes a problem when you have them frequently.

- Explain Personalizing. Then have students look at the worksheet example.
- Explain the remaining types of negative thinking patterns and have students fill in their own examples on the worksheets.
- Discuss how negative thoughts lead to negative moods.
- Help students create a challenge for each negative thought.

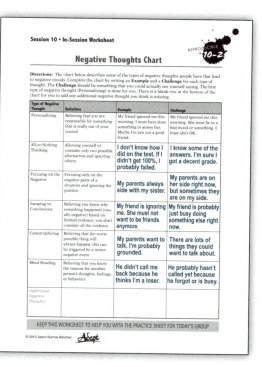

178   How Do I Manage My Negative Mood?

SESSION 10

4 **Hand out the Activities That I Enjoy worksheet (Reproducible 10-3).** Guide students through the worksheet, and explain that you can lift a negative mood by doing things you enjoy.

Have students circle their favorite activities, then write in additional activities they enjoy. Ask students to share their favorite activities, and write those activities on the whiteboard.

5 **As time permits, guide students through a negative mood management role-play.**

- Explain the importance of practice.
- Identify a common trigger for a negative mood. Then have students role-play using the trigger, negative thoughts, challenge to the negative thought, and a pleasant activity to lift the negative mood.

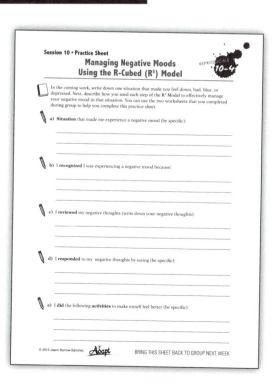

ENDING THE SESSION

1 **Have students clarify what they learned.**

Ask students what they found most helpful about negative mood management skills and how they might use them in the future.

2 **Pass out the Session 10 Practice Sheet, Managing Negative Moods Using the R-Cubed (R³) Model (Reproducible 10-4).**

Remind students that their practice sheets are due at the beginning of the next session, where they will be reviewed in the group.

ADAPT: Advancing Decision Making and Problem Solving for Teens   179

SAMPLE SESSION

BEGINNING THE SESSION

1 Welcome students.

2 **Review last session's practice sheets.** Discuss two or three student practice sheets.

- Ask students what they learned about anger management from the assignment.
- Thank students and encourage them to continue to use the anger management skills in their daily life.

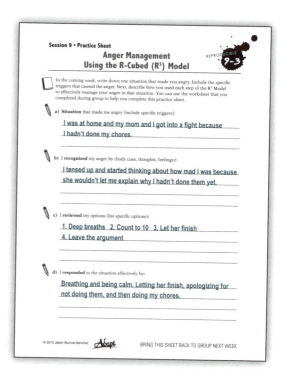

PRESENTING THE TOPIC & PRACTICING SKILLS

Mood Management Skills

1 **Introduce the topic of mood management.** Explain that brief negative moods are normal.

Last week we discussed how everyone experiences anger. Today we're going to discuss negative moods. Like anger, negative moods are also something everyone experiences. If you are depressed, down, blue, or sad, it's a negative mood. Experiencing negative moods for brief periods of time is normal.

- Ask the students how they describe negative/depressive moods.

  You may describe this experience differently, so I want to know how you label it. I'll write your examples on the board. Who would like to start? Megan? Do you mean like when I'm feeling depressed?

  Exactly. Some of you may not call it feeling depressed. It's like being bummed out.

  OK. What are other examples?

How Do I Manage My Negative Mood?

SESSION

10

- Explain that negative moods that get worse or last a long time are problems.

  A negative mood is normal if it is short, but it can become a problem if it doesn't go away or gets worse. If that happens, you may need to talk to a school counselor, nurse, therapist, psychologist, or another professional who can help you feel better.

  If any of you feel like you've been experiencing a negative mood for a long time or it seems to be getting worse, please talk to me. I can connect you with someone who can help. People who are feeling down often just don't know how to improve their mood.

- Explain that negative moods can lead to bad decisions.

  A negative mood not only makes you feel bad, but it can also lead to poor decision making and problem solving. It's hard to make good decisions when you are feeling down.

- Explain that negative moods can be managed.

  Occasional negative moods usually begin during adolescence and can continue into adulthood. In general, girls are at higher risk for experiencing negative moods and depression than boys. With time, a negative mood often goes away on its own. However, this isn't always true, so it's important to have skills to deal with negative moods.

  Think about the last time you felt down or depressed and answer the question: "Was it harder to do things?"

  Who would like to share a time when you felt down or depressed and what it felt like? Angie? Well, about three weeks ago, my boyfriend and I broke up. I felt pretty bad for a while.

  Can you give a little more description about how you felt? I didn't want to do anything. I had a hard time getting up in the morning to go to school. My friends tried to make me feel better, but it really didn't work.

  How are you doing now? A lot better. I finally realized that I shouldn't be wasting my time being depressed about him.

  When people are down, they may do things like stay in bed all day, isolate themselves, or take drugs. They think those things will help. Typically, these types of things don't work but only make the mood worse.

  There are things that people can do to feel better. We are going to discuss specific skills you can use in order to feel better. First, let's discuss why we experience negative moods in the first place.

> **IMPORTANT NOTE**
> **Suicidal Thoughts**
>
> If a student shares suicidal thoughts or intent, pull the student aside as soon as possible to provide referrals and immediate support. Depressed students will almost always be grateful for the support of a caring adult. Be sure to follow any applicable state and district guidelines.

ADAPT: Advancing Decision Making and Problem Solving for Teens

SESSION 10

SAMPLE SESSION

2 **Direct students to the Mood Model on the board (or the display of Reproducible 10-1).** Explain that the model will help them understand why people experience negative moods.

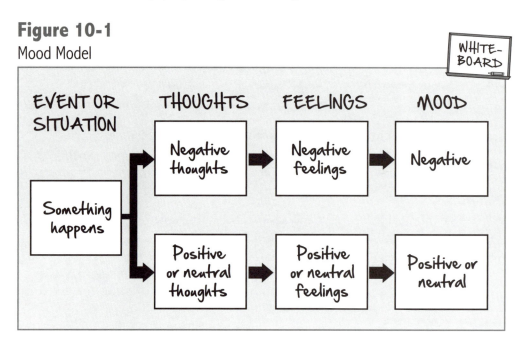

Figure 10-1
Mood Model

Let's take a look at the model on the board. This model will help us understand why people experience negative moods.

The model shows that first you experience a situation. That is, something happens. **Point to the appropriate portion of the model as you describe it.**

Second, you have thoughts about that situation.

Third, you have feelings about that situation.

Fourth, you experience a mood that is related to that situation and your subsequent thoughts and feelings after the situation happened. So your mood is not determined by the situation only, but also by the thoughts and feelings you had about it.

The model shows that our mood is influenced by what we think and feel about a situation. It also shows that we can experience a negative mood or a positive or neutral mood for the same event.

A neutral mood means that you don't really feel good or bad about something, but somewhere in between. A neutral mood does not make you feel bad. Only the negative mood makes you feel bad.

Look at the model. Do you think the situation, thoughts, or feelings are most important in causing a negative mood? Maria? I think feeling bad is the worst thing.

Feeling bad is an outcome. What do you think causes you to feel bad? The event?

How Do I Manage My Negative Mood?

Events are like a trigger. Your thoughts about a situation usually determine how you will feel about it. So, it's actually negative thoughts that lead to a negative mood. The exact same situation can end up making you feel two different ways, depending on your thoughts about it.

For example, say you get robbed. If you tell yourself, "Oh, I'm so happy I didn't get hurt," you may end up feeling grateful or just neutral. If you tell yourself, "Oh, no. I lost all my money. I won't be able to pay my bills," you may end up feeling down. So your perception of an event is as important as the event itself in determining how you end up feeling about it.

Let's take a look at this model more closely and see how this works.

- Work through Martin's Parent Criticism Scenario, filling in the top row of the blank Mood Model as you go (see Figure 10-2 below for Martin and Sam's completed scenarios).

Figure 10-2
Martin and Sam's Parent Criticism Scenario

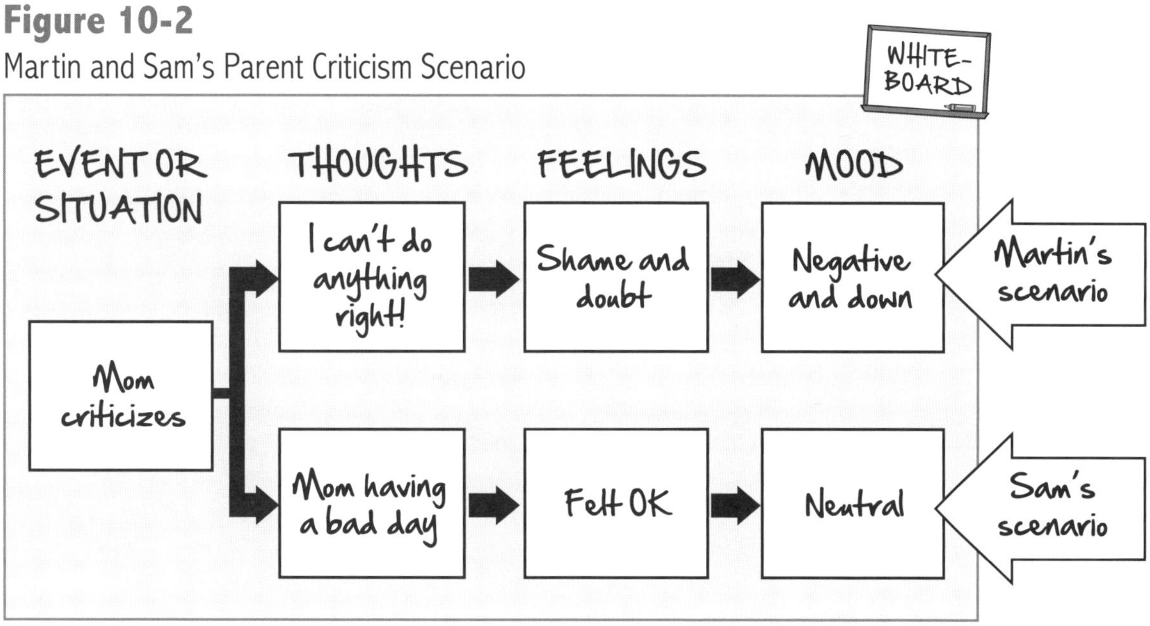

As you can see, I drew a blank Mood Model on the board. We are going to fill it in using an example. Our first example is about a student named Martin who felt bad because his mom yelled at him for watching TV and not doing his homework. I'm going to write "Mom criticizes" in the first box.
Write "Mom criticizes" in the Event box.

This situation led Martin to have the following thoughts:

- *Mom doesn't like me.*
- *She thinks I'm stupid and lazy.*
- *I can't do anything right.*

ADAPT: Advancing Decision Making and Problem Solving for Teens   **183**

SAMPLE SESSION

I'm going to write the last thought in the Thoughts box in the top row. **Write "I can't do anything right!" in the Thoughts box in the top row.**

These thoughts led Martin to have feelings of shame and doubt. I'm going to write that in the Feelings box in the top row. **Write "Shame and doubt" in the Feelings box on the top row.**

These feelings led Martin to feel down about himself. **Write "Negative and down" in the Mood box on the top row. Label the top row "Martin's Scenario."**

- Emphasize the need for students to stop and think about negative thoughts because they occur so quickly.

  Most of us don't stop and think about why we are feeling a certain way—we just find ourselves feeling that way. Think about the last time someone criticized you and made you feel bad.

  Did you stop and say, "What thoughts am I having about being criticized?" No, you probably jumped right to feeling bad, which led to a negative mood. Does this make sense to everyone? Ryan? Yeah, actually a teacher snapped at me yesterday. She was upset with me because I didn't get my assignment in. She said I was wasting my potential. I felt bad afterwards and still do. I felt like she was disappointed in me and that I was letting her down.

  So you jumped right to feeling a certain way about yourself and didn't ask yourself why you might be feeling that way? Yeah, I guess so.

  Kind of like Martin? Yeah.

  In Martin's example, he experienced the feelings so quickly that he didn't recognize the thoughts that came before them. When this happens, it is called having automatic thoughts. You experience the feelings so quickly that you lose track of the thoughts that caused them. Unfortunately, these automatic thoughts are negative. They lead to experiencing negative feelings and ultimately result in a negative mood. That is exactly what happened to Martin. Using this model, it is easy to understand why Martin ended up experiencing a negative mood. What questions do you have so far? Ryan? So, this is kind of like what I did?

  Yes, it's similar. The main thing is that you didn't stop and think about why you were feeling a certain way by examining your thoughts about the teacher saying something negative to you, which was the event. This is normal. Most of us don't stop and think about why we are feeling a certain way. We just find ourselves feeling that way.

- Work through and compare Sam's Parent Criticism Scenario, filling in the blank Mood Model as you go. As you work through Sam's scenario, discuss how his reactions are different from Martin's, even though the trigger is the same. Emphasize that it is Martin's negative thoughts and not the event itself that led to his negative mood.

184   How Do I Manage My Negative Mood?

SESSION

10

Now let's fill in the bottom row as we work through the model with Martin's brother, Sam. Their mom also yelled at Sam for watching TV and not doing his homework. **Point to "Mom criticizes" in the first box of the model.**

Sam's thoughts after the event were: "Mom must have had a bad day at work again. I wonder if her boss was on her case. We always watch TV before we do our homework. It isn't like we don't get our work done." In other words, Sam did not take the criticism from his mom personally. Instead, he looked for reasons why his mom may have acted that way. Sam concluded that his mom was having a bad day. **Write "Mom having a bad day" in the Thoughts box on the bottom row.**

Sam's thoughts did not lead to him feel bad about himself. Instead, he felt OK because he didn't take the criticism personally. I'm going to write that in the Feelings box. **Write "Felt OK" in the Feelings box on the bottom row.**

Sam ended up feeling neutral, not really positive or negative. The situation did not lead to bad feelings and a negative mood. **Write "Neutral mood" in the Mood box on the bottom row. Label the row "Sam's Scenario."**

As you can see, Sam had very different thoughts than Martin did about the same event. What do you think about this model and the differences between their thoughts? Ryan? *So, if I would have thought differently about what my teacher said, I would have felt better about it?*

Yes, that's a distinct possibility. Megan, it looks like you have a question? *A comment. See, if a teacher told me what she told Ryan, I would think that the teacher cares about me and really wants me to do well. That's why she is being hard on me. I think it would motivate me to do better.*

What do you think your mood would have been like? *Probably a little down because I had disappointed the teacher, but not negative. I think I would want to do better. I would probably be more energized to show the teacher I can do it.*

What you're saying is that having a different perspective about the situation can lead to different outcomes in terms of mood? *Yeah, I guess so.*

That's exactly what happened in the case of Martin and Sam. They both experienced the same event but perceived it in different ways. They had different thoughts about it and that led them to feel differently about it. In this model, the key is to recognize automatic negative thoughts so you can stop and challenge them because they can really influence how you feel about things.

You can't always control the situations that trigger the negative thoughts that then lead to negative moods. Martin and Sam didn't have control over their mom's criticizing them. Their automatic thoughts led immediately to how they felt. Because these thoughts happen so quickly, it can be hard to completely prevent them from happening. But if you practice, you can develop the habit of challenging negative thoughts, and feel more positive about situations in general. That's what we'll discuss next.

ADAPT: Advancing Decision Making and Problem Solving for Teens   **185**

SESSION 10

SAMPLE SESSION

3 **Hand out the Negative Thoughts Chart (Reproducible 10-2).** Tell the students they will learn about different kinds of negative thoughts that can lead to negative moods and also how to challenge those negative thoughts. Explain that having negative thoughts from time to time is normal, but it becomes a problem when you have them frequently.

So we learned from Martin's scenario that negative thoughts can create negative moods. Look at the worksheet I just passed out. Remember, just like anger, having negative thoughts from time to time is normal. It becomes a problem when you have these types of thoughts frequently.

- **Explain Personalizing. Then have students look at the example.**

  Take a look at the chart on your worksheet. The first column lists types of negative thoughts. The second column defines those ways of thinking. The third column gives an example, and the last column shows a challenge to that way of thinking. Let's look at the first type of negative thought.

  Personalizing occurs when you think you are responsible for something that is out of your control. I call this the "everything is about me" thought.

  Examples of Personalizing thoughts are:

  - *My friend ignored me. I must have done something wrong. Maybe I'm just not a good friend.*
  - *The teacher never encourages me. It's because I'm a bad student.*
  - *My parents are always arguing. If I was a better son, they wouldn't argue. It's my fault.*

  With these thoughts, you feel responsible for negative events that may have nothing to do with you. These thoughts cause you to feel bad about yourself.

  The example on the worksheet is, "My friend ignored me this morning. I must have done something to annoy her. I'm just not a good friend." The challenge to that thinking is, "My friend ignored me this morning. She must be in a bad mood. I hope she'a OK."

- Explain All-or-Nothing Thinking. Then have students write an example on their worksheets.

  All-or-Nothing Thinking is when you only consider two options that are the opposite of each other. All-or-Nothing Thinking is the opposite of brainstorming. Examples of this type of thinking are:

  - *I'm either going to ace this test or fail it.*
  - *People either like me or hate me.*
  - *I'm going to study for this test all night or not study at all.*

  The problem is not seeing other options. There are a lot of grades you can get on an exam besides an A or an F. People can have different degrees of like or dislike for you, rather than just liking or hating you. You also have many options for how

186 *How Do I Manage My Negative Mood?*

long to study for a test—some is better than none. When you limit yourself to only two options, you usually end up feeling hopeless about the situation, which leads to a negative mood.

Please take a minute and fill in an example on your chart of All-or-Nothing Thinking. We'll do challenges to the negative thoughts later.

- **Explain Focusing on the Negative. Then have students write an example on their worksheets.**

  Focusing on the Negative ignores positive things that may have happened. You can think of this as wearing dark glasses as opposed to rose-colored glasses. You see things as dark or negative, with very little positive.

  Examples of this type of thinking are:

  - *"My teacher wrote two negative comments on my paper. She never has anything good to say about my writing." The student thinks this even though the teacher wrote seven positive comments on the paper.*
  - *"I got a B on this quiz. I never do well in this class." The student says this to himself even though he received As on all the other quizzes in the class.*
  - *"My parents are mad at me again for being late. They never tell me when I do things well." This student ignores the fact that her parents often praise her for things she's done.*

Focusing on the negative doesn't allow you to see the "big picture" or consider all the evidence. Focusing on the negative prevents you from seeing what's positive in a situation. It can leave you feeling that bad things always happen to you. You may feel that nothing will ever change and that you don't have control over things. All of this leads to a negative mood.

Please take a minute and fill in an example of Focusing on the Negative on your chart.

- **Explain Jumping to Conclusions. Then have students write an example on their worksheets.**

  Jumping to Conclusions is when you believe that you know why something happened, but your conclusion is based on limited evidence. You can think of this as the "negative know-it-all." Examples of these types of thoughts are:

  - *"I got a C on this test. I'm going to fail this class." This student ignores the fact that she has an A in the course and that a C on a test will not put her in jeopardy of failing class.*

ADAPT: Advancing Decision Making and Problem Solving for Teens   **187**

- *"The school counselor called my parents today, and I know he said bad things about me."* This student ignores the fact that there can be many reasons why the school counselor called his parents.
- *"My girlfriend didn't call last night. I know she is mad at me."* Again, there can be many reasons why this student's girlfriend didn't call.

These types of thoughts lead you to believe you already know why something happened and prevent you from considering any other possibilities. These thoughts usually leave you feeling like things will always turn out bad for you and can lead to negative moods.

Please take a minute and fill in an example on your Negative Thoughts chart.

- **Explain Catastrophizing. Then have students write an example on their worksheets.**

Catastrophizing is when you believe that the worst possible thing will always happen. Thoughts of the worst possibilities can be triggered by a minor negative event. These thoughts include things like:

- *"Bad things always happen to me."* This person ignores all of the good things that have happened.
- *"My girlfriend didn't call me last night. She is definitely going to break up with me."* This person ignores that there could be many reasons why the girlfriend didn't call.
- *"My teacher wants to talk with me after class. I know she is going to tell me that I'm not going to pass this class."* This student ignores the fact that she is doing really well in the class.

The problem with thinking this way is that you consider only the worst possible outcomes and do not recognize that other, better outcomes are also possible. These negative thoughts leave you feeling like you are doomed and have no control over how things are going to turn out. The negative thoughts lead to a negative mood.

Fill in an example of Catastrophizing on your chart.

- **Explain Mind Reading. Then have students write an example on their worksheets.**

Mind Reading is when you believe that you know the reasons for another person's thoughts, feelings, or behavior. These types of thoughts include such things as:

- *"I know why my boyfriend is acting distant. He is going to break up with me."* In this instance, the student ignores that her boyfriend has been having a hard time at home.
- *"That person rarely says 'Hi' to me. It's because he doesn't like me."* This student doesn't consider that the person may be shy and doesn't say "Hi" to many people.
- *"My teacher didn't say anything nice to me today. She is disappointed in me for some reason."* That teacher could just be having a bad day.

188   *How Do I Manage My Negative Mood?*

These types of thoughts are a problem because you assume that you know the reasons why another person is acting a certain way without any real evidence. Once again, the negative thoughts leave you feeling bad about yourself and powerless to change the situation.

Please fill in an example of this type of thinking on your chart.

- Discuss how negative thoughts lead to negative moods.

   What are your overall reactions to the types of thoughts we just discussed? Do these thoughts make sense to you? Do you understand how they are related to negative moods?

   Megan? Yes, they make a lot of sense. I've never thought about it that way before. I think I spend more time than I should focusing on the negative.

   What about you, Jamal? Yeah, I use mind reading all the time. I always think I know what people are thinking.

- Help students create a challenge for each negative thought.

   The last column in the worksheet asks us to challenge the negative thought to see if it is really accurate or not. When we challenge a negative thought, we often find that it is not accurate. Some of the questions we can ask ourselves to challenge a negative thought include:

   - *What makes this thought true? or What makes this thought untrue?*
   - *What evidence do I have to prove this thought is true or untrue?*
   - *Have I had a similar thought before? Was it true?*
   - *Would my best friend think this thought was true if I asked him or her?*
   - *What is a more reasonable thought to have instead of this one?*

   I want you to take a couple of minutes to write down challenges to each type of negative thought on the worksheet. The first one—Personalizing—gives you an example.

 Hand out the Activities That I Enjoy worksheet (Reproducible 10-3). Guide students through the worksheet, and explain that you can lift a negative mood by doing things you enjoy.

I just passed out the Activities That I Enjoy worksheet. Listed on the worksheet are a number of things that people enjoy doing and that make them feel good. Research has shown that when people are feeling down or sad, doing something like exercise or another pleasant activity tends to make them feel better. The problem is that most people don't want to do things when they are feeling sad or down. So, this is an especially important time to challenge yourself to do something that will make you feel better, even if you don't want to.

Have students circle their favorite activities, then write in additional activities they enjoy. Ask students to share their favorite activities, and write those activities on the whiteboard.

SESSION 10

SAMPLE SESSION

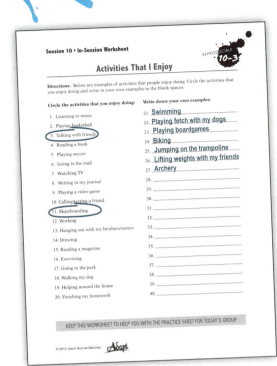

On the left-hand side of the worksheet, I want you to circle things that you enjoy doing and that typically make you feel better. On the right-hand side of the worksheet, write down your own examples.

Now I want you to share some of the examples you circled or wrote down. As you share them, I will write them on the board. Who would like to start?

Megan? *I circled talking with friends and writing in my journal.* Good!
What about you, Will? *Basketball, taking my dog on a walk, and going to my cousin's house . . .*

Great! There are a lot of things to choose from that make people feel better. It's important to remember that all things may not work for everybody, so each of you needs to identify the pleasant activities that work for you.

5 **As time permits, guide students through a negative mood management role-play.**

- Explain the importance of practice.

  We learned that negative thoughts, feelings, and moods happen rapidly, or automatically. To manage those moods, it's good to practice.

- Identify a common trigger for a negative mood. Then have students role-play using the trigger, negative thoughts, challenge to the negative thought, and a pleasant activity to lift the negative mood.

  Your friend is mad at you because you don't have time to meet her at the mall. Angie and Maria, would you do a role-play with that? Sure.

  Angie, would you like to be the angry friend? OK.
  Maria, you will want to tell us your negative thoughts and then how you will challenge those thoughts.

  Angie: Maria, you are so stupid. You just don't care about me. I really wanted to go to the mall.

  Maria: I am a bad friend. I feel bad. I let you down. I should skip doing my homework and come with you, but I just can't.

  Oops, no. It isn't reasonable to go to the mall instead of doing my homework. That doesn't have anything to do with our friendship.

  Angie, here is an alternative. I like going to the mall, too. Let's go on Saturday.

190 How Do I Manage My Negative Mood?

SESSION 10

ENDING THE SESSION

1 **Have students clarify what they learned.**

Ask students what they found most helpful about negative mood management skills and how they might use them in the future.

Before we end today, I want to know what you thought about the mood management skills we discussed. Specifically, what things do you like about them and what things may be hard to do?

2 **Pass out the Session 10 Practice Sheet, Managing Negative Moods Using the R-Cubed (R³) Model (Reproducible 10-4).**

I've handed everyone their practice sheets. To complete this practice sheet, you will be using an R-Cubed Model similar to the one we used to manage anger. That is, Recognize, Review, and Respond. The R-Cubed Model works for managing negative moods as well.

Choose one situation in the coming week in which you experience a negative mood. First, describe the situation that led to the negative mood. Be as specific as possible in your description. Second, describe how you used the R-Cubed Model to effectively deal with the situation.

This will include describing how you recognized you were experiencing a negative mood. See if you can figure out some body cues. Then identify the negative thoughts and feelings. List some of your options for challenging your negative thoughts and some favorite activities you might do.

Finally, describe your response—how you challenged your negative thoughts and the activity that you did. You can use the two worksheets you completed in group today to help you with the practice sheet.

Remind students that their practice sheets are due at the beginning of the next session, where they will be reviewed in the group.

SESSION REFERENCES

Depression Model: Monti et al., 2002; Webb et al., 2002.

R-Cubed Model: Webb et al., 2002.

Negative Thoughts: Auerbach, 1997; Beck et al., (1979); Beck (1995); Webb et al., 2002.

Activities that I Enjoy: MacPhillamy & Lewinsohn, 1982.

ADAPT: Advancing Decision Making and Problem Solving for Teens   **191**

HOW DO I GET THE SUPPORT I NEED FROM OTHERS?

SESSION 11

Session Goals

- Students learn that getting support from others is normal and helps people deal better with stressful situations.
- Students learn effective skills for obtaining social support for themselves.
- Students review listening skills and problem-solving skills for providing social support to others.

Session Preparation

1. Quickly review the Session Outline.
2. Study the Sample Session and sample dialogue to help you anticipate how your students might respond to content.
3. Draw the Social Support Circle diagram (see Reproducible 11-1) on the whiteboard, or plan to display Reproducible 11-1. Make sure you are familiar with the Social Support Circle worksheet.

Materials

- Presentation copy of Social Support Circle (Reproducible 11-1)
  Note: Project on a document camera or enlarge (129% on 11" x 17" paper).
- For each student, one copy of:
  - Social Support Circle (Reproducible 11-1)
  - Session 11 Practice Sheet, Getting Support From Others (Reproducible 11-2)
- Whiteboard and dry-erase markers
- Pencils for students to use during session

ABOUT THIS SKILL

Everyone needs social support from others. Students learn that asking others for support typically leads to better outcomes. Knowing how to ask for support will make students feel that they are not all alone in solving their problems.

SESSION OUTLINE

BEGINNING THE SESSION

1 Welcome students.

2 Review last session's practice sheets.
- Review two or three student practice sheets.
- Ask students what they learned about managing negative moods from the assignment.

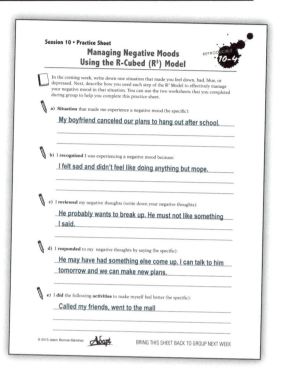

PRESENTING THE TOPIC & PRACTICING SKILLS

Social Support Skills

1 **Introduce the topic of social support.** Explain to students that needing social support is normal and that other people can help you to solve difficult problems.

2 **Pass out the Social Support Circle worksheet (Reproducible 11-1).** Use the worksheet to teach students how to obtain social support by identifying supportive people and the types of support each can provide. (*Note*: You can display the worksheet and fill it in with your responses while students complete their own copies.)
- Tell students that at times of stress, it is more difficult to ask for help, so this exercise will help them be prepared.
- Have students write their names in the center circle.
- Have students write the names of support people they know well in the middle circle. This might include family members, friends, and teachers.

194 How Do I Get the Support I Need From Others?

- Have students write the names of support people they know less well in the outer circle.
- Have students identify and write next to each person's name the kind of support that person can provide. For example, being a good listener, giving advice or guidance, and/or providing encouragement.
- Have students draw a circle around the names of the top two support people in each circle.

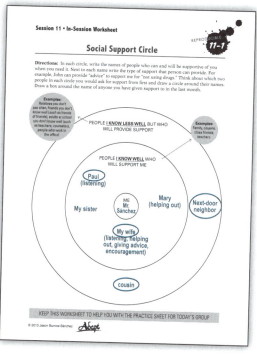

3 **Demonstrate how to obtain social support by going through a student's Social Support Circle on the whiteboard.**

- Write a student volunteer's name in the center circle on the whiteboard, then write his or her top two support people in the appropriate circles.
- Ask the volunteer these questions about each support person:
  1. How do you know the person?
  2. What type of support might you go to the person for?
  3. How would you ask for support?
- Continuing to use the Social Support Circle example, review with students how assertive communication works best for getting their needs met.
- As time permits, repeat the activity with other student volunteers.

4 **Have students draw a box around anyone they've supported in the last month on their Social Support Circle worksheets.** Explain to students that people who are good at supporting others also tend to develop strong networks of support for themselves.

- Have students review the listening skills: Listen, Clarify, and Recap.
- Review problem-solving options from Session 2: brainstorming, giving yourself advice, thinking about advice from others, and thinking about past problems. Tell students one way they can provide support is by sharing these strategies with others.

5 **As time permits, have students role-play getting and giving support.** Provide positive, descriptive feedback as students use the skills they have learned.

ADAPT: Advancing Decision Making and Problem Solving for Teens   195

SESSION OUTLINE

6 Summarize.
- Review how to obtain social support.
- Encourage students to practice getting and giving social support in their daily lives.

ENDING THE SESSION

1 Have students clarify what they learned.

Ask students what they found most helpful about obtaining social support and what they think may be hard to do.

2 Pass out the Session 11 Practice Sheet, Getting Support From Others (Reproducible 11-2).
- Walk students through the practice sheet.
- Remind students that their practice sheets are due at the beginning of the next group session, where they will be reviewed in the group.

196 How Do I Get the Support I Need From Others?

SAMPLE SESSION

SESSION 11

BEGINNING THE SESSION

1 Welcome students.

2 Review last session's practice sheets.
- Review two or three student practice sheets.
- Ask students what they learned about managing negative moods from the assignment.

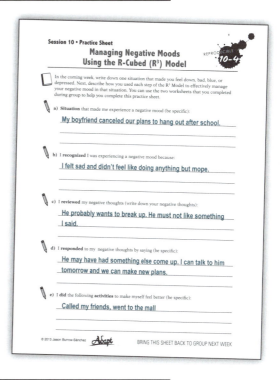

PRESENTING THE TOPIC & PRACTICING SKILLS

Social Support Skills

1 **Introduce the topic of social support.** Explain to students that needing social support is normal and that other people can help you to solve difficult problems.

We all need support from other people in our lives. We call this social support. Other people can help us solve difficult problems more effectively than if we try on our own. Researchers have found that people deal with stressful situations better with help from others. Social support can help each of us feel better and is something we all need.

Even though we know help is good, there are many reasons people don't ask for help. Some of us have been taught that we should solve problems on our own. We may think that no one can understand our situation, or that we look weak or stupid if we ask for help. Sometimes, we don't ask for help because we are embarrassed.

Even though you may have some of these feelings, it is important to ask others for support in solving difficult problems. Most people ask for help and need help from time to time. I don't know anyone who has solved every single problem on his or her own So today we are going to talk more about getting support and giving others support.

ADAPT: Advancing Decision Making and Problem Solving for Teens

197

SESSION 11

SAMPLE SESSION

2 **Pass out the Social Support Circle worksheet (Reproducible 11-1).**
Use the worksheet to teach students how to obtain social support
by identifying supportive people and the types of support each can
provide. (*Note*: You can display the worksheet and fill it in with your
responses while students complete their own copies.)

- Tell students that at times of stress, it is more difficult to ask for
  help, so this exercise will help them be prepared.

  *Because we don't always have the support we need, we can sometimes feel like
  we are all on our own. The good news is this: We can get social support from a
  variety of people, including friends, family, and acquaintances. We can also learn
  how to increase the amount of social support we have in our lives.*

  *The first step is to be aware of the people who can provide support to you. During
  times of stress, it is more difficult to ask for support or help, so it's good to think
  ahead.*

  *The worksheet I just passed out will help you identify people who can support you
  and the kinds of support you can ask them for.*

  As you see from the worksheet, there are three circles.

- Have students write their names in the center circle.

  The center circle is you. Write your name in that circle.

- Have students write the names of support people they know well in
  the middle circle. This might include family members, friends, and
  teachers.

  *The middle circle is for people you know well who can provide you with support.
  Look at the examples in the small gray circle of people you know well. They
  include family, cousins, close friends, and teachers. Some of the people I am
  putting in my circle are my wife, my sister, and my good friends Paul and Mary.*

  *Go ahead and write the names of people you know well who would provide you
  with support in the middle circle.*

- Have students write the names of support people they know less well
  in the outer circle.

  *The largest circle is for people you know less well but who could still provide you
  with support. Examples include distant relatives, acquaintances and friends you
  don't know well, and adults at school who you don't know well. This could include
  teachers and administrators. Some people I don't know quite as well but who
  would provide support if I needed it are my next-door neighbor and my cousin
  who is a counselor.*

198 *How Do I Get the Support I Need From Others?*

SESSION 11

- Have students identify and write next to each person's name the kind of support that person can provide. For example, being a good listener, giving advice or guidance, and/or providing encouragement.

    The types of support you might ask for include things like listening, getting advice, receiving encouragement, or getting help. List the ways each person might help you. For example, on my map I'm going to put "listening" next to Paul, "helping out" by Mary, and all of those things plus "giving advice" and "encouraging me" next to my wife.

    Do this for the middle and outer circles. Any questions before you start? Angie? Yeah, is this kind of like a map?

    Kind of—it helps you identify the people who are supportive in your life. Does that make sense? Yeah.

    Will? What if we don't have too many people to put down?

    Put down as many people as you can and don't worry about the number. Each of us will have a different number of people in our life who can provide support.

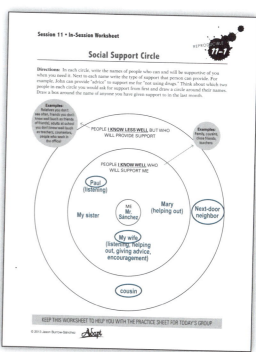

- Have students draw a circle around the names of the top two support people in each circle.

    Now I want you to draw a circle around the names of the two people in each circle you would go to first for support. I'm going to circle my wife and my best friend, Paul, in the middle circle. In my outer circle, I'm going to circle my neighbor and cousin—because they are the only ones I listed in that outer circle.

3 **Demonstrate how to obtain social support by going through a student's Social Support Circle on the whiteboard.**

- Write a student volunteer's name in the center circle on the whiteboard, then write his or her top two support people in the appropriate circles.

    OK, so now you have a list of people who can give you support, and we've thought a little about what kind of support they can provide.

    Let's go back to getting support for ourselves. Let's use the diagram on the whiteboard to practice how to get support from others. I need one of you to volunteer by sharing the examples you wrote on your worksheet. Will? OK, I guess.

    Thanks. I'll write your name in the center of the circle. Next I'll write the two people you drew a circle around in the middle circle, then the two you identified in the outer circle.

ADAPT: Advancing Decision Making and Problem Solving for Teens   199

SESSION 11

SAMPLE SESSION

- Ask the volunteer these questions about each support person:
    1. How do you know the person?
    2. What type of support might you go to the person for?
    3. How would you ask for support?

    In the middle circle, you identified James as someone who you would ask for support. First, who is James and how do you know him? He's my stepbrother.

    What type of support would you go to James for? Probably listening to me, mostly, but sometimes he has good ideas. We have to deal with the same problems.

    How would you ask James for support? I'd just tell him I'm bummed out, and then we would talk about it.

    That's excellent. It sounds like you and James have great communication.

- Continuing to use the Social Support Circle example, review with students how assertive communication works best for getting their needs met.

    OK, great. Give me the name of someone you circled in your outer circle. Mr. Johnson.

    He's our counselor. Have you ever talked to him before? No, we were just told he was our counselor. Isn't that what counselors are for?

    Absolutely. What kind of support might you ask him for? I guess school problems, like how to make up credits.

    How would you ask him for help? I don't know. I've never talked to the guy.

    *Let's think about some of the things we learned about in Session 8.
    We learned you could be aggressive, passive, indirect, or assertive in the way you communicate.*

    Do you think you could get help by being aggressive? Like in his face? Probably not.

    How about indirect? Megan? Well, if Will didn't tell him what he needed help with, it would be kind of hard to help him. *That's exactly right.*

    So, what would assertive look and sound like, Will? I guess I would just tell him I wanted help making up credits. *That's great. It would be more like what you do with your stepbrother. You can often get help by simply saying what you need to the right person.*

200   *How Do I Get the Support I Need From Others?*

- As time permits, repeat the activity with other student volunteers.

   Angie, do you have an example? Yes. I had Ms. Smith down in my outer circle— but I wasn't sure where to put her. I guess actually she could be in the middle circle.

   There's no right or wrong about where you place someone. We know Ms. Smith is a math teacher. Is she your teacher? She isn't my teacher this year, but I don't get math this year and I did OK last year with her.

   Good, so you are finding math hard this year and you need help? Many of us find math hard to do without help. One of the reasons you would go to Ms. Smith is that she's been helpful in the past.

   How would you ask Ms. Smith for help? It would be like we talked about with Will. I would take her my math homework and ask her if she could help me understand it better.

   Great. That's a great example of being direct and using assertive communication. Does anyone in the group want to add comments or suggestions about how to handle a situation like this?

   Thanks for helping me with that exercise. From the material we covered today I hope all of you have a clearer picture of the people in your lives who you can ask for support.

4 **Have students draw a box around anyone they've supported in the last month on their Social Support Circle worksheets.** Explain to students that people who are good at supporting others also tend to develop strong networks of support for themselves.

Now I want you to draw a box around the name of anyone, in either the middle or outer circle, you have given support to in the last month. If you think of people you supported who are not in a circle yet, add their names.

Look at the names you've drawn a box around. In general, we find that someone who is good at providing support is also good at asking for support.

If you see a lot of boxes on your sheet, you are probably good at both giving and asking for support from others. However, if you don't see many boxes on your worksheet, you may want to think about trying to be more supportive of others when they ask for it.

Giving support to others doesn't mean that you have to their solve problems. It means that you can do anything from being a good listener to providing suggestions to giving advice or encouragement.

SESSION 11

SAMPLE SESSION

- Have students review the listening skills: Listen, Clarify, and Recap.

  If you are giving support to someone else, you can use the listening skills we learned in Session 8. Do you remember what you do? First, you listen with your body facing the other person. Then what? Ryan? Umm, I think it was something about asking questions.

  Yes, excellent. You ask questions to make sure you understand. What's next? Maria? I remember now. You repeat what you heard. I don't remember what that was called.

  We called that Recap. But it doesn't matter what it's called. The important thing is you remembered what to do.

- Review problem-solving options from Session 2: brainstorming, giving yourself advice, thinking about advice from others, and thinking about past problems. Tell students one way they can provide support is by sharing these strategies with others.

  If you are providing support but are not sure what to do, you can be a good listener. You can also share some of the strategies we learned for problem solving. For example, you could ask yourself, "If it was my problem, what would I do?"

  What other options did we practice for problem solving? Maria? Well, we brainstormed. I remember that was really a big help to me when I goofed and broke curfew. My parents were really angry, so I brainstormed ways that I could earn back their trust.

  Excellent. If that helped you, it might help a friend who came to you for support. We also talked about thinking about past problems. How might that help you support a friend? Jamal? I could tell a friend how I got out of trouble.

  OK, so we've talked about providing support by listening, brainstorming, and thinking about what we might have done and sharing that. Jamal added thinking about past problems and sharing how those were handled. I think the only thing we missed was thinking about advice that others might give us. You have a great set of options for solving your own problems and providing support to others.

5 **As time permits, have students role-play getting and giving support.** Provide positive, descriptive feedback as students use the skills they have learned.

Let's brainstorm a list of common problems that you might need support for. Then we'll do a little role-playing of how you would get support and give support.

Here's the first situation you came up with. Your boyfriend or girlfriend has lied to you and is going out with your best friend. Who would like to be in that role-play? Jamal? Sure, as long as you know that hasn't happened to me.

202 How Do I Get the Support I Need From Others?

Look at your worksheet. Who would you go to for support? My friend here, Ryan.

Ryan, looks like you are up for the other part in the role-play.

Jamal, tell us how you would get support. Bad situation, man. I just found out Monica has been sneaking around with Stewart.

Ryan, go ahead and respond.

Ryan: Tell me what happened.
Jamal: I saw them at the store. They were holding hands.
Ryan: What did you do?
Jamal: I walked away.
Ryan: Bad stuff. Were you angry?
Jamal: I was really pissed, but I walked away.
Ryan: That was smart. That must have been hard to do. What are you going to do next?
Jamal: That I don't know.
Ryan: What are your options?

Ryan and Jamal, I'm impressed. Let's think about what's happened so far. Megan, what did Jamal do to get support? He told Ryan what the problem was.

Yes, Jamal did a very effective job of getting support from Ryan. And what is Ryan doing to provide great support? Angie? Well, he is listening. He's facing Jamal and making eye contact. And now he's asking questions.

That's right. Ryan is helping Jamal clarify what happened. Shall we continue or do a different role-play. Angie? I think they should continue. I'd like to see what they come up with.

 Summarize.

- Review how to obtain social support.

  Everyone needs the support of others when dealing with difficult situations. In general, people with good social support tend to do better dealing with difficult problems and situations. We identified people in your lives you can turn to for support and the types of support you might ask them for.

  You can get support by having someone listen, offer suggestions, give advice, or encourage you. Asking for support is usually best done with an assertive communication style so that the other person knows what you want and need.

  In addition, people who provide support to others are usually better at asking others for support. I'm impressed with the ways you are able to use the skills we've learned to help yourselves and others.

ADAPT: Advancing Decision Making and Problem Solving for Teens

SESSION 11

FACILITATOR'S STUDY GUIDE

- Encourage students to practice getting and giving social support in their daily lives.

  Remember to keep practicing the skills we learned today in your daily lives. It is important that you make these skills work for you, and you need to practice them in order to do that.

ENDING THE SESSION

1 **Have students clarify what they learned.**

Ask students what they found most helpful about obtaining social support and what they think may be hard to do.

2 **Pass out the Session 11 Practice Sheet, Getting Support From Others (Reproducible 11-2).**

- Walk students through the practice sheet.

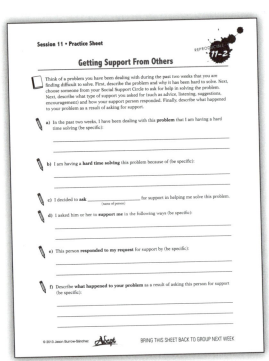

I've handed everyone a practice sheet called Getting Support From Others. This sheet requires you to describe a problem you have been dealing with in the past two weeks and that you are having a difficult time solving. Be as specific as possible in your description.

Next, you will need to describe why the problem has been difficult to solve and then pick someone from your worksheet to ask for support in solving it.

Then you will describe the type of support you asked for and how the person responded to your request.

Finally, you will describe what happened to your problem as a result of getting support. For example, did your problem get solved completely, partially, or not at all?

Are there any questions?

- Remind students that their practice sheets are due at the beginning of the next group session, where they will be reviewed in the group.

SESSION REFERENCES

Depue, 1982; Marlatt & Witkiewitz, 2005; Monti et al., 2002; Webb et al., 2002.
In-session worksheet: Webb et al., 2002.
Practice Sheet: Monti et al., 2002; Webb et al.

How Do I Get the Support I Need From Others?

Ending the Program & Additional Support

SESSION 12

Session Goals

- Students review the skills they learned over the course of the program.
- Students discuss strategies for obtaining post-group support.
- Students are empowered to share their experiences with the program.

Session Preparation

1. Quickly review the Session Outline.
2. Study the Sample Session and sample dialogue to help you anticipate how your students might respond to content.
3. Identify school and community resources for support. Add these to the Resource List (Reproducible 12-2; fillable PDF) before copying for group members.
4. Customize the Certificate of Participation (Reproducible 12-3) for each student.
5. Optional Closing: Share an observation about each student's growth and a goal for continued work. Think in advance about what you will share with each student. You may wish to review student's original goals from their contracts.

Materials

- For each student, one copy of:
  - ADAPT Skills Review (Reproducible 12-1)
  - Resource List (Reproducible 12-2)
  - Participation Certificate (Reproducible 12-3)
- Whiteboard and dry-erase markers
- Pencils for students to use during session

ABOUT THIS SKILL

Students review skills they've practiced, used, and benefited from. Post-group support is covered because students will need continued help to maintain growth and to keep making gains. Finally, students are asked to provide positive and constructive feedback about ADAPT.

GENERALIZATION

One goal of Session 12 is to encourage students to generalize the support skills learned in ADAPT to other school, community, and personal resources. Students may want to continue to meet, either as a group or with you individually. In such cases, refer the students to other resources available in the school or community and work with them as needed to make connections with those resources.

Encourage students to stay in touch once the group has ended, especially if they run into difficulty obtaining support from other resources. However, limit such meetings to a brief check-in. They should not turn into individual counseling sessions.

Booster sessions can be helpful and should be open to all group members and planned from the beginning of the program. See p. 19 for details on including optional booster sessions one to two months after the group has ended.

SESSION 12

SESSION OUTLINE

BEGINNING THE SESSION

1 Welcome students.

2 Review last session's practice sheets.

- Review two or three student practice sheets.
- Ask students what they learned about getting support from others from the assignment.

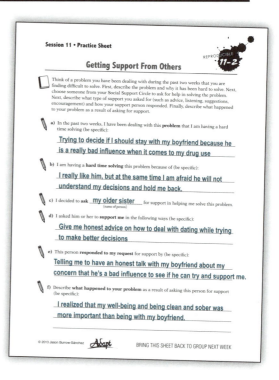

PRESENTING THE TOPIC & PRACTICING SKILLS

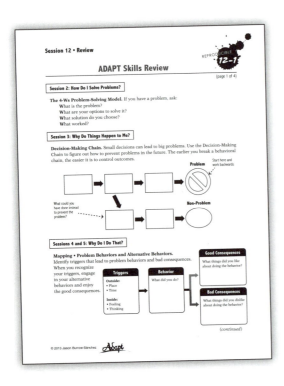

Skill Review and Additional Support

1 Tell students that it is normal to feel a sense of loss when the group ends.

2 Review the skills learned during the program. Hand out ADAPT Skills Review (Reproducible 12-1).

- Briefly review the topics covered in each session, eliciting examples from students of what they have learned.
- Ask students to share two skills they learned in the group and how those skills have helped in their daily lives. Write skills on the board.

206   *Ending the Program and Additional Support*

3 **With students, problem solve how they will obtain the support they need once ADAPT ends.** Students often underestimate the level of support they received from the group, so it is important that they know how to obtain the resources they need once the group has ended.

- Pass out the Resource List worksheet (Reproducible 12-2) that you filled out before group to students.
- Ask students to share their personal experiences with any of the resources listed on the worksheet.
- Brainstorm additional resources with the students and have them add these resources to their lists.
- Remind students of the people they identified in the last session who can support them. Have students add those people to their lists.

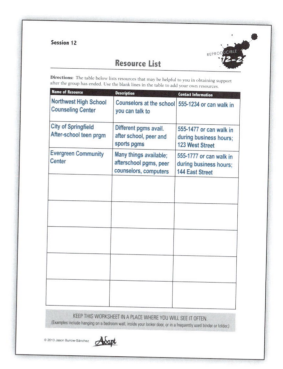

4 **Ask students to share their feedback about ADAPT.** The opportunity to provide feedback empowers students.

- Ask students to share one positive thing about their participation.
- Ask students to share ways in which ADAPT can be improved. *Note*: Some students will be hesitant to share negative or constructive feedback about ADAPT. If this happens, use prompts such as:
  - I want to know if there was anything you didn't like about the group.
  - I'd like to know what didn't work for you.
  - Think back to when the group started. Was there anything that bothered you?
  - Are there any specific things we talked about that you wish we hadn't discussed?

ADAPT: Advancing Decision Making and Problem Solving for Teens

SESSION 12

SESSION OUTLINE

ENDING THE SESSION

1 **Optional closing exercise: Share an observation about each student's growth and a goal for continued work.**

For each student, share one observation of growth you have seen over the course of the program. Also share a goal for continued growth. Your feedback provides an opportunity for praise and a constructive suggestion for future growth.

2 **Conclude the session by passing out the Certificates of Participation (Reproducible 12-3), congratulating students, and inviting them to stay in touch.**

- As you pass out certificates, congratulate students individually for participating and thank them.
- Invite students to stay in touch with you.

Ending the Program and Additional Support

SAMPLE SESSION

SESSION 12

BEGINNING THE SESSION

1 Welcome students.

2 Review last session's practice sheets.
- Review two or three student practice sheets.
- Ask students what they learned about getting support from others from the assignment. Conclude with something like:

  Remember that most people are more effective at solving difficult problems when they have the support of others. Continue to practice the social support skills we learned in your daily lives.

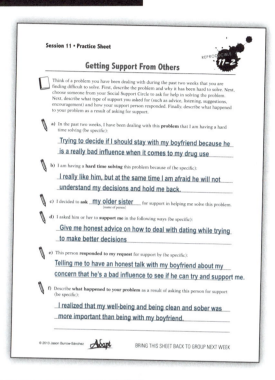

PRESENTING THE TOPIC AND PRACTICING SKILLS

Skill Review and Additional Support

1 **Tell students that it is normal to feel a sense of loss when the group ends.**

As you know, today is our last session. We have spent the past 12 weeks learning a lot of skills that I hope each of you has found useful.

Our time together has gone by quickly. I enjoyed our sessions—getting to know one another and discussing the many topics we covered. You may have mixed feelings about the group ending. You may feel glad because you are done with the program but sad because this group provided you with support. Mixed feelings are normal when finishing a program like this. Feel free to tell us how you feel about the group ending during today's session.

We have three things to accomplish today. First, we'll briefly review what you have learned. Second, we will discuss how you can get additional support after the group ends. Finally, I want to get your feedback about your experiences in ADAPT—what things you liked and what things you think could be improved. This information will help me make improvements for the next group of students who participate in the program. Let's get started.

ADAPT: Advancing Decision Making and Problem Solving for Teens

SESSION 12

SAMPLE SESSION

2 **Review the skills learned during the program.** Hand out ADAPT Skills Review (Reproducible 12-1).

- Briefly review the topics covered in each session, eliciting examples from students of what they have learned.

    We've covered a lot of material during the program and learned some useful skills. Take a look at the ADAPT Skills Review sheet I handed out.

- Ask students to share two skills they learned in the group and how those skills have helped in their daily lives. Write skills on the board.

    I'd like you to think of two skills you learned in the group and how those skills have helped you in your daily lives. As you share examples, I will write them on the board. Who would like to begin? Maria? Well, I learned how to talk with my mom better, and now we don't get into arguments.

    Great. What specific skills are you referring to? I have tried listening more to what my mom is saying, and I've also asked her to listen to what I am saying.

    So you have tried asking for what you need—part of being assertive—and using listening skills? Yes.

    How has it been working for you? Actually, pretty well —I mean, we still argue but not like it was.

    It sounds like the skills have been helping but that there is still some work to do to improve the communication with your mom? Yes, and I want it to get better.

    Great example, Maria!

    Repeat with each student in the group.

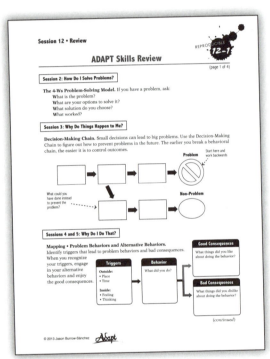

3 **With students, problem solve how they will obtain the support they need once ADAPT ends.** Students often underestimate the level of support they received from the group, so it is important that they know how to obtain the resources they need once the group has ended.

- Pass out the Resource List (Reproducible 12-2) that you filled out before group.

    I want to discuss how each of you can get additional support now that the group is ending. Some of you may not feel like you need additional support after the group ends, but some of you may.

Remember, there are always ways to get additional support. We're going to look at some ways to get support in the community, at school, and from people in your Social Support Circle. Examples could include attending a program at the community center, connecting with one of our after-school programs, and talking with the school counselor, a friend, family member, or teacher.

Whatever the case, I want each of you to know there are resources. To begin our discussion, I've listed some places that I know about on your Resource List. You'll see the name of the resource, a description of what is provided, and contact information. You can add notes on the back of the sheet.

- **Ask students to share their personal experiences with any of the resources listed on the worksheet.**

  Have any of you used any of the resources listed on the worksheet?

  For those of you who have used them, did you like what they provided? Do you think the resource could be useful for others in the group?

  I appreciate you sharing your experiences about the resources you've used.

- **Brainstorm additional resources with the students and have them add these resources to their lists.**

  I also want to discuss other resources at our school or in the community that are not on the resource list. Are there some that you know of and would recommend? Let's spend a few minutes brainstorming some additional resources. I will write your suggestions on the board. Who would like to start?

  Work with students to generate a list of possible resources on the board and ways to access them.

  Add these resources to your Resource List worksheet.

- **Remind students of the people they identified in the last session who can support of them. Have students add those people to their lists.**

  Last week, you completed your Social Support Circle. Some of the people you identified were people who have been supportive in the past. Take a few minutes to add the names of your highest ranked social support people to your Resource List.

Session 12

Resource List

REPRODUCIBLE 12-2

Directions: The table below lists resources that may be helpful to you in obtaining support after the group has ended. Use the blank lines in the table to add your own resources.

Name of Resource	Description	Contact Information
Northwest High School Counseling Center	Counselors at my school I can talk to	555-1234 or I can walk in
City of Springfield After-school teen prgm	Different pgms avail. after school, peer and sports pgms	555-1477 or can walk in during business hours; 123 West Street
Evergreen Community Center	Many things available; afterschool pgms, peer counselors, computers	555-1777 or can walk in during business hours; 144 East Street

KEEP THIS WORKSHEET IN A PLACE WHERE YOU WILL SEE IT OFTEN.
(Examples include hanging on a bedroom wall, inside your locker door, or in a frequently used binder or folder.)

© 2013 Jason Burrow-Sánchez

ADAPT: Advancing Decision Making and Problem Solving for Teens

SESSION 12

SAMPLE SESSION

 Ask students to share their feedback about ADAPT. The opportunity to provide feedback empowers students.

As we end our group, I want to know what you liked about ADAPT and what should be changed. As we discuss these things, I want you to be honest. I don't want you to worry that you are going to hurt my feelings if you say something you think I don't want to hear.

It is important for me to know the good things about our sessions as well as the things you think should be improved. Your feedback will help me improve the program for the next group of students.

- Ask students to share one positive thing about their participation.

    Let's start with everyone sharing one thing they like about ADAPT. I'll start. I liked how much everyone participated in the sessions. Who would like to go next? Megan? I liked how I got to know everyone in the group.

    Say more about what you mean. Well, everyone had a chance to talk rather than you just lecturing us. That happens a lot in class. I liked that I got to hear from everyone about what was going on with them.

    Great, thanks for sharing.
    Repeat with each student in the group.

    Thanks to everybody for sharing those positive things about the program.

- Ask students to share ways in which ADAPT can be improved. *Note*: Some students will be hesitant to share negative or constructive feedback about ADAPT. If this happens, use prompts such as:

    - I want to know if there was anything you didn't like about the group.
    - I'd like to know what didn't work for you.
    - Think back to when the group started. Was there anything that bothered you?
    - Are there any specific things we talked about that you wish we hadn't discussed?

    This next part can be a little more difficult, but I'm sure everyone can handle it. I want to know what ways you think the program should be improved. Remember, this type of information is important for me to know so I can improve the program for future students. Who would like to start? Ryan? Well, I kind of think the group should be longer. I mean we only go for 12 sessions, but maybe it could be longer during the school year—kind of like a class.

    OK, you think this program could be improved by meeting for a longer period of time—like for the school year? Yes.

Ending the Program and Additional Support

That's a good suggestion, Ryan. Do others think the program should be longer? Jamal? Yeah, that sounds like a good idea.

Ryan, thanks for sharing your suggestion for improvement. Lengthening the program is something I will consider, and it sounds like others share your thoughts.
Repeat with each student in the group.

I want to thank everyone for sharing positive and constructive feedback about the program. This information is very helpful, and I will make sure to consider it as I prepare for the next group of students who participate in the program.

ENDING THE SESSION

1. Optional closing exercise: Share an observation about each student's growth and a goal for continued work.

For each student, share one observation of growth you have seen over the course of the program. Also share a goal for continued growth. Your feedback provides an opportunity for praise and a constructive suggestion for future growth.

Before we end today, I want to say what a pleasure it has been to work with each of you over the course this program. I have seen each of you learn and grow in different ways. I have also noticed things that each of you can continue working on. Your growth across the time we've spent together tells me you will succeed in the future.

I would like to spend just a few minutes sharing how I've seen each of you grow and my suggestion for further growth.

I'll start with Angie. When you first started the group, I remember that one of your goals was to improve your performance in school. Specifically, you said that you were having trouble with one teacher who you felt didn't listen to you and this was causing problems. When we discussed ways to improve communication skills, you tried to be more assertive with this teacher in a respectful way. You tried to be more direct in order to feel that you were being heard. Recently, you've said this teacher seems to be listening more and things have been better in the class. I am really glad that things have improved for you, and I'm proud of the way you've used the skills we worked on. Does what I've said sound accurate to you?

Allow the student the opportunity to agree, disagree, or provide corrections to what you have said.

Angie, you have also said that communication with your dad hasn't improved much, but you are committed to keep trying. I'm confident that things will get better with your dad if you keep working at it by using the skills we learned in the group. Does this sound accurate to you?

Allow the student the opportunity to agree, disagree, or provide corrections to what you have said.

SAMPLE SESSION

2 **Conclude the session by passing out the Certificates of Participation (Reproducible 12-3), congratulating students, and inviting them to stay in touch.**

- As you pass out certificates, congratulate students individually for participating and thank them.
- Invite students to stay in touch with you.

  Before we end today, I want to give each of you a Certificate of Participation. I want you to know that I have really enjoyed working with each of you. If you ever need to contact me for some reason, you can find me in office 32 at our school. I hope you will stop by periodically and update me on how you are doing.

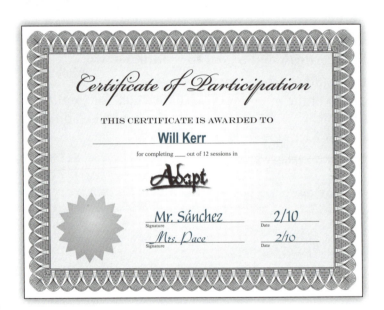

Ending the Program and Additional Support

RESEARCH SUMMARY

Many of the techniques and strategies used in this program are based in cognitive-behavioral intervention literature and have been tested in treatment studies for adult and adolescent substance abusers. However, many of the strategies used in those studies have broader application beyond the substance abuse treatment setting and, therefore, were modified for use in the ADAPT program. In particular, four research-based substance abuse treatment manuals were utilized during the development and adaption process for the program: *Treating Alcohol Dependence: A Coping Skills Training Guide* (Monti et al., 2002), *Cognitive-Behavioral Coping Skills Therapy Manual* (Kadden et al., 1992), *Motivational Enhancement Therapy and Cognitive Behavioral Therapy for Adolescent Cannabis Users: 5 Sessions Manual* (Sampl & Kadden, 2001) and the *Motivational Enhancement Therapy and Cognitive Behavioral Therapy Supplement: 7 Sessions of Cognitive Behavioral Therapy for Adolescent Cannabis Users* (Webb, Scudder, Kaminer, & Kadden, 2002). In addition to these manuals, other intervention-based resources were used from the professional and research literature and included in the program.

How was the ADAPT program developed and tested in a school setting?

The ADAPT program is based on the Building and Enhancing Skills for Teens (BEST) program that was developed and tested during a two-year pilot study. The initial year of the pilot study was funded by a one-year seed grant awarded to Jason Burrow-Sánchez, Ph.D., and Mandy Allison, M.D., from the Adolescent Health Initiative program in the Department of Pediatrics at the University of Utah. Funding for year two of program development and testing was supported by the Utah State Office of Education and the American Academy of Pediatrics (Healthy People 2010 Grant). The goals for pilot testing the intervention program included establishing procedures for recruitment/retention, measuring social validity (e.g., participant satisfaction), and examining indicators of efficacy.

The distribution of students across grade levels (9–12) and gender was fairly even during both years of the study. Approximately 60% of the students across both years reported racial/ethnic backgrounds other than White, with the largest non-White subgroup being Hispanic/Latino. The

215

SUMMARY

satisfaction scores across both years were generally high for students, teachers, and parents. For example, most participants indicated that they found the program worth their time and effort and that they would recommend it to others.

Outcomes for the pilot study included substance use levels, depressive symptoms, and self-esteem scores. Scores were calculated for students in the BEST condition who attended at least eight sessions or more, which was considered a reasonable level of exposure to the intervention. Late into the data collection process it came to the researchers' attention that students at pre-test (BEST and control conditions) and post-test (control condition only) were most likely underreporting their drug use. It was hypothesized that this was caused by student discomfort with providing self-report drug use information in a school setting. In contrast, students at post-test in the BEST condition were more likely to accurately report their drug use because they had already been exposed to the program for 12 weeks; thus, these students trusted that their drug use information would not be shared outside of the research program. These hypotheses were also supported through corroboration by some students who had completed the intervention. For this reason, only post-test drug use information for students in the BEST condition across both years is reported here; there were no validity concerns for the other outcome measures.

Drug Use

On average, 76% and 59% of students in the BEST condition across both years reported they had not used alcohol or marijuana, respectively, in the month prior to completing the program. Alcohol and marijuana are two of the most frequently used substances by adolescents, and past month use is generally considered an indicator of "regular" or "current" use in national surveys. Thus, these percentages indicate that well over half of the students who participated in the BEST program reported being abstinent from either alcohol or marijuana during the month prior to the end of the intervention. Of course, the reader needs to keep in mind that these post-test percentages are not compared with substance use outcomes from the control condition due to the validity concerns mentioned above; however, these percentages provide an indication of substance use levels at post-intervention for those students who participated in the program.

216

Depressive Symptoms

On average, students reported fewer depressive symptoms at post-test in the BEST condition compared with students in the control condition across both years. The average effect size across both years was -0.1917 in favor of those in the BEST condition. This can be interpreted to mean that depressive symptom scores for the average person in the BEST condition were 0.1917 standard deviations below the scores for the average person in the control condition. Stated another way, the average person who participated in the BEST program reported fewer depressive symptoms than approximately 60% of those in the control condition.

Self-Esteem Symptoms

On average, students reported higher self-esteem scores at post-test in the BEST condition compared with students in the control condition across both years. The average effect size across both years was 0.5524 in favor of those in the BEST condition. This can be interpreted to mean that self-esteem scores for the average person in the BEST condition were 0.5524 standard deviations above the scores for the average person in the control condition. In other words, the average person who participated in the BEST program reported higher self-esteem scores than approximately 70% of those in the control condition.

Conclusion

Taken together, the results from the two-year pilot study were very promising, indicating that students who participated in the BEST program generally had better outcomes than those in the control condition. The results also indicated that students, teachers, and parents perceived the program to be worthwhile and helpful for the students who participated in it. In addition, the researchers found that school personnel positively embraced the program, which helped in generating student referrals and sustainability over the two-year development and testing period.

REFERENCES

American Psychiatric Association (2000). *Diagnostic and statistical manual of mental disorders—text revision* (4th ed.). Washington, D.C.: Author.

American Psychological Association Zero Tolerance Task Force (2008). Are zero-tolerance policies effective in the schools? An evidentiary review and recommendations. *American Psychologist, 9,* 852–862.

Auerbach, S. (1997). *Clean and coping manual.* Unpublished.

Beck, A. T., Rush, A. J ., Shaw, B. F., & Emery, G. (1979). *Cognitive therapy of depression.* New York: Guilford Press.

Beck, J. S. (1995). *Cognitive therapy: Basics and beyond.* New York: Guilford Press.

Bedell, J. R., Archer, R. P., & Marlow, H. A. (1980). A description and evaluation of a problem-solving skills training program. In D. Upper & S. M. Ross (Eds.), *Behavioral group therapy: An annual review.* Champaign, IL: Research Press.

Burr, W. R. (1990). Beyond I-statements in family communication. *Family Relations, 39,* 266–273.

Burrow-Sánchez, J. J., & Hawken, L. S. (2007). *Helping students overcome substance abuse: Effective practices for prevention and intervention.* New York: Guilford Press.

Corey, M. S., & Corey, G. (2006*). Groups: Process and practice* (7th ed.). Belmont, CA: Thomson/Brooks/Cole.

Depue, J. (1982). Getting a little help from your friends. In J. Depue (Ed.), *Managing stress* (Pawtucket Heart Health Program treatment manual, pp. 1–9). Pawtucket, RI: Memorial Hospital.

D'Zurilla, T. J. & Goldfried, M. R. (1971). Problem solving and behavior modification. *Journal of Abnormal Psychology, 78,* 107–126.

Erford, B. T. (2010). *Group work in schools.* Upper Saddle River, NJ: Pearson Education.

Erford, B. T., Eaves, S. H., Bryant, E. M. & Young, K. A. (2010). *35 techniques every counselor should know.* Upper Saddle River, NJ: Pearson Education.

Geroski, A. M., & Kraus, K. L. (2010). *Groups in schools: Preparing, leading, and responding.* Upper Saddle River, NJ: Pearson Education.

Greenburg, K. R. (2003). *Group counseling in K-12 schools: A handbook for school counselors.* Boston: Allyn & Bacon.

REFERENCES

Kadden, R. M., Carroll, K., Donovan, D., Cooney, N., Monti, P., Abrams, D., M. Litt, & Hester, R. (Eds.). (1992). *Cognitive-behavioral coping skills therapy manual: A clinical research guide for therapists treating individuals with alcohol abuse and dependence* (Vol. 3). Rockville, MD: National Institute on Alcohol Abuse and Alcoholism.

Marlatt, G. A., & Witkiewitz, K. (2005). Relapse prevention for alcohol and drug problems. In G.A. Marlatt & D.M. Donovan (Eds.), *Relapse prevention: Maintenance strategies in the treatment of addictive behaviors.* New York: Guilford Press.

MacPhillamy, D. J., & Lewinsohn, P. M. (1982). The pleasant events schedule: Studies on reliability, validity and scale intercorrelation. *Journal of Consulting and Clinical Psychology, 50,* 363–380.

Miller, W. R., & Rollnick, S. (2002). *Motivational interviewing: Preparing people to change addictive behavior.* New York: Guilford Press.

Monti, P. M., Kadden, R. M., Rohsenow, D. J., Cooney, N. L. & Abrams, D. B. (2002). *Treating alcohol dependence: A coping skills training guide.* New York: Guilford Press.

Mrazek, P. J., & Haggerty, R. J. (Eds.). (1994). *Reducing risks for mental disorders: Frontiers for prevention intervention research.* Washington, DC: National Academy Press.

Myers, R. J., & Smith, J. E. (1995). *Clinical guide to alcohol treatment: The community reinforcement approach.* New York: Guilford Press.

National Institute on Drug Abuse (2011). *Drug facts booklet.* Retrieved from http://drugfactsweek.drugabuse.gov/files/teenbrochure_508.pdf

National Institute on Drug Abuse (n.d.). *Easy-to-read drug facts.* Retrieved from http://www.easyread.drugabuse.gov/index.php

National Institute on Drug Abuse (n.d.). *NIDA for teens.* Retrieved from http://teens.drugabuse.gov/

National Institute on Drug Abuse (n.d.). *Parents and teachers.* Retrieved from http://www.drugabuse.gov/parents-teacher

National Institute on Drug Abuse (n.d.). *Student and young adults.* Retrieved from http://www.drugabuse.gov/students-young-adults

Reilly, P. M., & Shopshire, M. S. (2002). *Anger management for substance abuse and mental health clients: A cognitive behavioral therapy manual* (DHHS Pub. No. (SMA) 03-3859). Rockville, MD: Center for Substance Abuse Treatment and Mental Health Services Administration.

Sample, S., & Kadden, R. (2001). *Motivational enhancement therapy and cognitive behavioral therapy for adolescent cannabis users: 5 sessions* (Cannabis Youth Treatment [CYT] Series, Vol. 1 [DHHS Pub No. (SMA) 03-3862]). Rockville, MD: Center for Substance Abuse Treatment, Substance Abuse and Mental Health Services Administration.

Sue, D. W., Carter, R. T., Casas, J. M., Fouad, N. A., Ivey, A. E., & Jensen, M. (1998). *Multicultural counseling competencies: Individual and organizational development* (Vol. 11). Thousand Oaks, CA: Sage.

Walker, H. M., Horner, R. H., Sugai, G., Bullis, M., Sprague, J. R., & Bricker, D. (1996). Integrated approaches to preventing antisocial behavior patterns among school-aged children and youth. *Journal of Emotional and Behavioral Disorders, 4,* 194–209.

Webb, C., Schudder, M., Kaminer, Y., & Kadden, R. (2002). *The motivational enhancement therapy and cognitive behavioral therapy supplement: 7 sessions of cognitive behavioral therapy for adolescent cannabis users* (Cannabis Youth Treatment [CYT] Series, Vol 2 [DHHS Pub. No. (SMA) 04-3954]). Rockville, MD: Center for Substance Abuse Treatment, Substance Abuse and Mental Health Services Administration.